CW00394000

SIGNALLING DAYS

Final Reminiscences of a Great Western Railwayman

by
Harold Gasson

Oxford Publishing Co · Oxford

©
1981 Oxford Publishing Co.

ISBN 0 86093 118 8

ACKNOWLEDGEMENTS

Writing a book is truly a labour of love to me, particularly when so many readers write expressing the wish for a continuation of my reminiscences. This can only be achieved with the help of others as it is essential for photographs to back up my written word.

Without the help from these good people, this book would lack that little extra, and I express my sincere thanks to the following:-

Jack Gardner, ex-Great Western Signalman
Ken Robinson, Photographic advice
Keith Barrow, ex-Great Western Fireman
Gordon Churchman, ex-Great Western Signalman
Brian Lowe, ex-Fleet Air Arm
George Nickson, Locomotive Dept, Bluebell Railway
Dave White, Locomotive Dept, Bluebell Railway
John Harmsworth, Locomotive Dept, Bluebell Railway
Peter Kelly, Editor, Steam Railway
The directors and staff of Oxford Publishing Company

This list, as always, must end with my dear wife, Betty, whose help is so valuable, her contribution to each book being almost equal to my own. Each page is handed to her for criticism, and although not many are rejected, those that are, prove beyond doubt, that she is usually right, and the finished work is much better for her evaluation.

Published by

Oxford Publishing Co.,
8 The Roundway,
Headington,
Oxford.

Introduction

With three books behind me I can now say with some authority that I enjoy writing, enjoy it enough to produce this fourth book, but only because of the many letters I receive from readers who write to me and ask 'When is the fourth book due out?'. Without those readers it would just not be worthwhile, so I say 'Thank you' for the encouragement that you have given me over the years, it *is* worthwhile to remember and to record those golden days of steam and signalmen, because that is what this book is all about.

'Firing Days', 'Footplate Days' and 'Nostalgic Days' are steam from beginning to end, but this book is a collection of reminiscences from my many years in the signal box together with some odd trips that I 'pinched' on the footplate.

Again I must thank my dear wife Betty for the unstinted help that she has given me with her valuable proof-reading, and the hours she has spent on her own while I bashed away on my old steam typewriter, and I thank my publisher, who has such faith in me, because without him there would be no 'Signalling Days'.

Harold Gasson,
1981

Contents

All rights reserved. No part of this publication may be reproduced, stored in a retrieval system or transmitted, in any form or by any means, electronic, mechanical, photocopying, recording or otherwise, without the prior permission of Oxford Publishing Company.

BRITISH RAILWAYS (W.R.)
"Block Telegraph Train Register" Book, for Double & Single Lines
UP TRAINS
B.R. 30213

Description of Train as Signalled	REPLY SENT "Is Line Clear?" through	Caution Station or Junction Blocked	"Is Line Clear?" sent	"Train out of Section" sent	REPLY RECEIVED "Is Line Clear?" through	"Train entering Section" sent	"Train out of Section" received	DELAYS
	ON DUTY 6.0am							
4.11.0 Chichester	6.14	16	.19	16	.19	.24		
3.05 Swindon	30 Goods Loop	.37	44	.37	40	46	Goods Loop	
4.6.15 Swindon	40	43	44	40	44	44		
3.40 Seven	7.16	23	27	23	27	33		
3.6.55 Swindon	34	41	43	34	41	46		
4.7.50 Swindon	8.18	21	33	18	33	46	Distant Check	
5.4.45 Taunton	26	30	33	26	33	55		
4.3.50 Stoke	33	40	45	40	45	46	Main to Goods Loop	
5.11 Soldadino	45	50	59	50	59	59	Main to Goods Loop	
4.7.0 Weston	59	9.1	3	9.1	3	6	Slip Direct	
4.7.5 Crass	9.18	22	22	18	22	31		
4.7.55 Fishguard	44	48	48	44	48	50		
4.7.55 Chert	49	53	51	49	53	55		
4.6.30 Swindon	55	59	59	55	59	10.1		
4.8.30 Bristol	10.6	9	8	9	8	9		
4.8.20 Weston	11	20	20	20	25	33	Main to Goods Loop	
4.4.45 Swindon	26	30	38	30	30	33	Slip Direct	
4.55 Fishguard	45	45	47	44	49	51		
4.06 Eckirson	11.3	3	9	3	12	14		
3.10.20 Swindon								
4.7.50 Taunton	12	15	16	15	19	26	Distant Check	
4.013 Eckirson	19	19	24	19	24	26		
3. Fey	24	28	30	28	30	44		
3.0 Rogerstone	30	37	40	37	40	56		
4.7.55 Carmarthen	49	54	51	49	56	56		
4.7.5 Stoke	12.3	9	13	9	13	41	Main to Goods Loop	
3.11.51 Swindon	27	30	32	27	36	44		
4.11.45 Bristol	45	44	47	45	47	49		
4.4.0 Exeter	1.10	50	54	50	52	33		
4.7.45 Penzance	51	53	33	53	36	34		
4.11.145 Chart	45	45	44	45	48	51		
4.8.0 Neyland	58	2.0	13	2.0	13	4		
	OFF DUTY 2.0 pm							

BRITISH RAILWAYS (W.R.)
"Block Telegraph Train Register" Book, for Double & Single Lines
DOWN TRAINS
B.R. 30213

Description of Train as Signalled	REPLY SENT "Is Line Clear?" through	Caution Station or Junction Blocked	"Is Line Clear?" sent	"Train out of Section" sent	REPLY RECEIVED "Is Line Clear?" through	"Train entering Section" sent	"Train out of Section" received	DELAYS
	ON DUTY 6.0 am							
4.1.15 Padd	3.9		17	.19	9	19	24	
3.11.0 o.o. con	20	Goods Loop	20	26	26	26	27	Goods Loop
4.1.18 Padd	33		38	41	33	41	43	
	Block instrument failure 8.33. Unable to Peg Line Clear to Fondall Set							
	Second Linesman advised 8.35. Arrived 8.50. Block restored 9.30							
4.1.55 Padd	3.0		4	6	3.0	6	8	
4.2.05 Padd	14		18	20	14	20	28	
3.2.32 Acton	26		28	31	28	31	37	
3.2.40 Bristol	35		35	48	35	48	49	
3.2.30 Bristol	54		57	4.1	54	4.1	4	
4.3.20 Padd	4.9		9	14	4.9	14	12	
4.3.45 Padd	44		48	51	44	50	57	
4.3.55 Padd	50		57	58	50	58	58	
4.4.45 Padd	5.15		15	19	15	19	20	
4.4.55 Padd	45		45	48	45	50	53	
3.5.0 Reading	6.2		6.0	14	6.2	6	8	
3.5.0 Reading	34		44	26	24	29	11	
4.5.16 Padd	37		37	37	34	37	40	
3.6.5 Scores Loop	49		57	51	57	38	38	
4.6.55 Padd	25		27	49	45	29	31	
4.6.30 Padd	38		43	44	38	44	46	
4.6.55 Padd	8.1		5	8	8.1	8	10	
4.7.5 Padd	14		18	20	14	20	22	
3.2 Vem Exmove	35		35	39	35	39	44	
3.1 Y48 Acton	9.0		55	3	9.0	3	5	
3.1.55 Grimsby	9.4 Goods Loop		4	10	Cancelled Down Goods Loop 9.7			
4.7.55 Padd	8		8	10	10	16	Loop — Main	
3.1.5 Grimsby	ex Goods Loop		11	5	10	11		
4.7.10 Hull	13		16	18	18	26		
4.7.45 Penzance	16		18	30	30	34	Distant Check	
4.9.0 Oxford	35		39	44	45	44	Distant Check	
3.9.18 Didcot	41		45	25	25	42		
	OFF DUTY 10.0							

Chapter One

The Parting

The pale December sunshine struggled bravely to inject some warmth and life into the dried and shrivelled dead heads of the late summer roses, covered now with a sugar coating of hoar frost.

It was just before two in the afternoon on a Monday as I made my way down the road towards the loco shed, feeling plump and contented with one of mother's large dinners under my belt, her suet pudding lying just under my belt buckle, heavy and solid enough to last a growing lad until the time came to snatch a hurried sandwich at Ranelagh Bridge later on, for I was on my way to prepare 5935 *Norton Hall* to work the 3.45 p.m. to Paddington. I was early by half an hour, as my booking-on time was 2.30 p.m. but with that dinner inside me I wanted a gentle preparation with time for that suet pudding to settle.

Noticing the hoar frost clinging to the lawns and privet hedges I realised gratefully that the cab would be a warm haven, for it had all the makings of a bitter cold evening. By the time we headed out of Didcot Station the sun would be spreading a crimson blanket over the horizon and the chill air would be beginning to bite, the oil thickening, the injectors on the point of hesitation as the water-feeds began to freeze, and the hands, alternating between heat and cold, would begin to split as the warm water softened the skin. Some firemen wore gloves to prevent this, and so did I when I had to lean out and catch single line tokens at speed, but for firing, it had to be bare hands, ever since the time when I lost the shovel in the firebox due to wearing gloves. After that, I put up with split thumbs and cracked knuckles, although the decision to handle buttons was something to ponder over and put off for as long as possible.

I walked into the Booking-On Hall and called out to Joe Hermon the Time Clerk that I was here for the 3.45 p.m. to Paddington, and he gave me the usual 'thumbs up', then he asked me to hold on for a moment. There was a shuffling round of various papers, then he produced a brown envelope and handed it to me; typed on the front was 'H. H. Gasson. Fireman. Registered No. 27297'. Letters for firemen were almost unheard of; we sometimes received notes, usually to report to the Foreman, for a change of duty, but letters could be a posting to far-away places, and out of the question for a young fireman in love! Well, there was only one way to find out, I had better do it now before my hands became covered in coal dust. I began to sweat as I opened that envelope and started to read, then all at once things began to fall into place, plans I had almost forgotten about.

This letter was to inform me that as from January 1st, my request for transfer from the Locomotive Department into the Traffic Department was to take effect, and that I was to report to the Reading School of Signalling for training at 8.0a.m.: a ticket was attached. There was a P.S. in the form of a warning, which stated that after the last turn of duty with the Locomotive Department all clothing and equipment from the said department must be returned to the stores, any items missing would be valued and that amount deducted from my wages. Some of my equipment was handed back of course, except for two gauge glasses, (handy for stirring paint) and one new set of overalls and cap, (which might come in handy one day, little did I know then that it would at Hereford and on the Bluebell Line), and of course I did need the new jacket and overcoat. The rest was handed in and checked off and such is administration, that I never did pay for those items I kept.

The prospect of receiving that letter had been tucked away in my mind for months, since it had been the previous March when I had applied for a transfer. I could have hung on and perhaps reached the driver's side of the footplate, because after all, that is what I had joined for, to drive a steam locomotive, but at the most, I would have had only a few years with steam locos being phased out as the diesels replaced them, and I had no inclination to spend the rest of my days driving those diesels. An additional spur to leave the footplate was the fact that so many other lads had gone before me, and had not regretted it.

At one time, once a man was accepted into the Locomotive Department it became his job for life, but the best years were now over, and the lads were leaving for better-paid jobs in pleasant environmental surroundings. Harwell R.A.F. Station had been handed over to the Atomic Energy Research people, and they welcomed ex-footplate men who could work without supervision, and alas the post-war boom had begun in the motor industry, Morris Motors and Pressed Steel at Cowley near Oxford were paying twice the amount that poor old British Railways Western Region could manage, and they too wanted good reliable men who could get up in the morning and do a fair day's work.

And they got them, good conscientious men who without exception, soon rose from the shop floor to become supervisors. Much later, when I joined them in factory life, I too became a supervisor.

With this drain of good men footplate life went downhill fast, lack of maintenance soon eroded the advantages that had been gained after the long hard Second World War. For the older men it was a case of sticking it out, and as for the younger men who stayed, they raised the last few years of steam to new heights, but I had decided regretfully that I would not hang on.

I had thought for a long time about what I could do; I could push a barrow on the platform, or hump sacks of wheat in the goods shed, but the eventual answer came from a neighbour, Jack Drew, who was a good friend and a good railwayman, when we were talking railways one day and he came up with the answer by inviting me to spend a couple of hours with him in Didcot North Junction signal box. Why not become a signalman, I thought! I had been in signal boxes many times to carry out Rule 55, all part of a fireman's duties, and on the whole they seemed a good lot of lads; boiling water for our tea can was never refused, and we paid by filling their coal bunker. There were of course the odd times when we were routed down a Goods loop which took the run out of a heavy freight train, and if it was a wet miserable day we were inclined to shout out that the box would benefit from a wire netting roof, but such insults were accepted in good spirit, and a signalman always replied with that most British salute of two fingers pointing skyways. On the whole, this signal box suggestion was worth looking into.

Some weeks later by a sheer fluke of luck the Shed Foreman forgot to book this young single lad for a Saturday duty, romance was out of the question because my young lady love was working, mother had no shopping for me to do, the 'old chap' had weeded the garden the day before, and the dog was asleep, so I was free, with time on my hands to squander, and off I went to Didcot North Junction. I slunk the long way round, through the goods yard, well out of the way of shed foremen and up the steps into the box. Jack was pleased to see me, for a signalman's life is a lonely one, and after the usual pleasantries, he began to explain the box workings. Bell signals were a complete jangle to me, although I could begin to follow through the frame by studying the diagram. Conflicting locking had me beat completely, but not to worry, this was a visit simply to assess a type of railway

3

working new to me, and by eight in the evening I knew I had been bitten by this signal bug: I loved it, at last I had found my niche in railway work outside the steam world, it was a job I knew I could get my teeth into.

As I left the box Jack pressed into my hand the signalman's 'Bible', the red book of signal box regulations, which was a condensed version from the Rules and Appendix with all the up-to-date amendments stuck inside. I took this book home and spent every spare minute reading through it. There was so much to learn, a lot of it of course overlapping the footplate rules, but still a tremendous amount to take in. Should I apply for a transfer, would I be making the right decision? I pondered over this for some weeks, meanwhile finding out that there were half a dozen of my old school mates in signal boxes scattered all over the district, now firmly entrenched, so visits were made, questions were asked, and once I was satisfied in my own mind beyond all doubt I took the plunge and applied for a transfer to the Traffic Department with the view of training for signal box duties.

The senior Shed Foreman, dear old Bill Young, was dismayed and held the application back for a few weeks while he tried to change my mind, for he had lost a lot of experienced firemen in the last few weeks. He got Bill Snow and Jack Jacobs, the two shift Foremen, to have a go at me, and the third Foreman, Ralph Painton (a shrewd move here because I had been Ralph's last fireman before he was promoted). Then Bill tried another tactic, he waited until my old Dad was booked as Shed Pilot driver, then took me off my booked duty and put me as Shed Assisting, now he had us both together and available. My old Dad had tried of course, saying that things would get better, steam would not go and so on, but in his heart he knew it would never again be the same as it was in his early days, so while Bill tried every argument to get me to change my mind the answer was the same. I think in a way perhaps Bill pushed me into refusing to withdraw that application when he pointed out that all my years on the seniority ladder would be thrown away, my service would count, but I would start at the bottom again, graded as a Porter. Well, we would see, it was a signalman that I wanted to become, and a signalman I would be, even a small box would do, then after a couple of years I would go after promotion and make up the lost years. If I had known then what was in store within those few years I think I might well have backed out, because I went into a main line box and within three years I had moved up to Class One

District Relief Signalman with a district of twenty-two boxes under my hat, but, I am going ahead of the story. The application went forward, through the misty channels of administration to Paddington via Swindon, and I waited and waited, through the summer months and the autumn, and still my name appeared on the duty roster, so I gave up and made the best of it, thinking that my application had been quietly put to one side, and that I would make enquiries in the New Year. When I opened that letter my emotions were all mixed up: shock, surprise, sadness and elation. I stuffed the letter in my pocket, climbed up onto the footplate of *Norton Hall* and set about raising steam, wishing that the suet pudding did not feel quite so much like a brick every time I bent down. After spreading the fire all over the box, I began to make up the fire with the excess coal that had been spilled all over the floor boards, and by the time my Driver Bill Darby arrived I had the cab clean and his oil feeder filled and laid on the ejector to warm, a little thing to do, but appreciated by drivers, who in turn would inspect the ash pan when underneath and so save me a chore, which was all part of working together as a team.

As we drifted up to the shed signal ready to leave, the doubts began to rise in my mind: six days to go, only six more engines to work on, no more Didcot, Newbury, Winchester, Southampton, no more Banbury, Swindon, Honeybourne, Gloucester, no more steam and the open road, for I would be stuck in one spot. The doubts began to ferment but as I wiped the sweat from my forehead, other thoughts began to work; no more dirt, no more 1.00a.m. starts, no more wondering if I would finish in time to meet my young lady, and the fact that I was leaving a failing world for a new life. In the last nine months I had spent hours in various signal boxes and I knew that given the chance I could cope with that kind of work; well, now I *had* been given the chance, and this time next week I would be in up to my neck. There was no time for brooding, now that I had burnt my bridges, and *Norton Hall* would be in no fit state if I didn't get cracking. I had a lovely fire burning through, about two feet thick all over the box, with three-quarters of a glass of water and the boiler pressure on the point of blowing off; I put on the live steam injector and knocked her back to 180lb, just long enough to keep her quiet in the station, because tannoys were not built to compete with Swindon safety valves blowing off. Then I began to fill up the back corners with the biggest lumps of coal I could find, knowing from experience that Bill drove in the Churchward manner, regulator up in the roof. We backed on to our ten coaches standing at number five platform and Bill eased up the pressure on the buffers so that I could lift the tender coupling over the coach hook, then I clamped together the vacuum and steam heating pipes, slid in the locking split pins, and returned to the footplate and opened up the valve to heat the coaches.

At 3.44 p.m. the signals began to tumble off, one after another from the platform, over the Up relief, and up the Main Line. There was a shrill whistle from far down the platform, Bill yanked at the whistle chain sending a tall column of steam into the frosty air as *Norton Hall* responded, then up into the cab roof went the regulator, and *Norton Hall* marched out of the station.

As we clattered over the points I could hear the faint 'ting! ting!' on the block bell, a sound that I had heard many times, but now I knew what it meant, we were 'On Line' to Moreton. The shadowy figures moving high up inside the signal box at Didcot East Junction were signalmen, and soon I would be one of them. Once clear of the junction Bill began to wind the reverser back, two turns only, and *Norton Hall* eased her strident bellow and settled down to an angry barking. The fire was roaring away, my big lumps dancing in tune; as I fired her, there was no need to aim for the front of the firebox, for the coal was snatched off the shovel as soon as the tip of the blade reached the fire hole ring. Bill had a reputation for fast hard running, and a 'Hall' being worked this way with ten thirty-five tonners tied on behind could scoff coal at an alarming rate. I worked hard to Southall, then it was time to let her go, because I would get no thanks for coming into Paddington with the engine blowing off. It was not until we ran in that the sound of the Great Western Band playing carols on the Green reminded me that it was Christmas Eve, since that letter had completely taken my mind off the Festive Season. As we waited for the Pilot to take away our coaches, the rasp of my shovel sounded almost indecent as I shovelled coal forward for the return journey.

We followed our coaches out, pausing only for the signal to be changed to allow us on to Ranelagh Bridge and the turntable. *Norton Hall* was quickly turned, we backed off the table, then while Bill squirted some oil round the motion I filled the tank, topping her up with a few hundred gallons of water. We now had half an hour to have a cup of tea and a sandwich, and to watch the world go by.

On the return trip, the 7.40 p.m. out of Paddington was packed to capacity with last-minute shoppers and people going home for Christmas, and we were pulling twelve coaches, fast as far as Slough, then stopping at all stations. Those extra coaches made our engine rattle and vibrate, finding all the loose bolts holding the cab down, so it was a relief to run into Cholsey knowing that this was the last stop before going to shed, although we would not be spending Christmas at home like the passengers we had carried.

Bill and I studied the special duty roster when we had finished with *Norton Hall*, and thought 'what a come-down for a Christmas Day', as we discovered that tomorrow we had to go to Newbury. We both booked on that next morning at 11.00 a.m. and prepared the old *Comet,* one of William Dean's old engines of 1899 vintage, but still going strong; she was in fact a powerful little engine, and one to be enjoyed, her only drawback for engine crews being the small cab, and the huge screw reverser that came so far back into the cab that the driver had to lean over the top of it.

We were off shed at 11.45 a.m. and into the goods yard where we picked up twenty assorted wagons and a brake van, agreeing with our guard that there seemed no earthly reason for the good people of Newbury to need this train on Christmas Day, and as we punched our way over the branch we bemoaned our luck, the only consolation being a higher rate of pay for the day, and a day off in lieu at another time. However, when we shoved our little train into the yard at Newbury the reason for our trip became clear, the signalman knew what the return working was, a train of empty coaches in the bay platform which were needed at Didcot, and although we could have come over light engine to pick them up, bringing that goods train over meant that the early morning goods the next day which was double-headed with two Collett 'twenty-two's' was now reduced in loading, so that would be one engine and crew saved. Clever blokes, Shed Foremen! We ran down to Newbury Race Course and turned the little *Comet,* picked up the empty coaches and set sail for home, booking off at 3.30 p.m. so it was a short turn and we still had part of Christmas Day left.

Boxing Day was another short turn, on duty at 1.30 p.m. to relieve some Old Oak Common men with a Down stopper. They ran in ten minutes late with 5004 *Llanstephan Castle* leaking steam from every joint, being badly in need of a Swindon overhaul. We had to nurse her along, so for once Bill did not use full regulator, and she was steaming so poorly that I could only use the injector when Bill shut off for stations, but somehow

Steventon, Wantage, Challow, Uffington and Shrivenham slipped by, and we were able to leave her on Swindon shed for a long-deserved rest.

The Foreman took kindly to us and told us to make our way home, so we caught the next Up train and were back home by five in the evening, both days having been messed about with short duties, a far cry from today's railway working, when the whole show shuts down. Friday brought a surprise when I arrived to prepare our engine for the 3.45 p.m. to Paddington, *Norton Hall* was at the rear of the shed waiting for attention from the fitters, then she would have a boiler washout, so, I had expected our other 'Hall' 6923 *Croxteth Hall* as that was the usual pattern, but instead, booked on the Duty Roster was 6973, a Churchward 'Mogul'.

I knew that she had been missing for a couple of months, and when a regular shed engine disappears it is usually because it has been lost in the pool of engines, and could be anywhere on the Great Western system, or might have gone to Swindon for overhaul, and this was the case, for I found her on number four road, gleaming with new paint.

I climbed up onto her footplate and just savoured her bright new cab; everything shone, the floorboards had been renewed and fitted tight, she even smelt right, all new and unsullied, a fireman's delight.

I had the fire burning up nicely and the new floorboards hosed off by the time Bill arrived, even he was excited about working on this new locomotive, although he was to change his mind before long. The first indication of difficulty came as we moved quietly up to the shed signal, her regulator was stiff, and it was a quiet departure, valves, piston, motions, axle boxes, all back to the original specification, with no wear anywhere, she rode like a Rolls, each rail joint sending up into the cab a distinct 'clunk, clunk'. We blew up over the points ready to set back on our coaches, then Bill placed his left foot up on the reversing quadrant foot support and heaved at the big lever. He got it halfway and dropped the clip down into the ratchet, his face turning red, and I had to give him a hand to place her into full reverse. Even I began to have doubts now, Bill was not a driver given to linking an engine back far anyway, what if we had full fore gear all the way? But I need not have worried, Bill was a canny bloke, and while I was busy coupling up, he was at work with the sight feed lubricator, so when I returned to the footplate those little oil blobs were going up the glass tube at a fair old rate.

8

We pulled away over the junction and up the Relief line, Bill shut off steam and together we linked her back just three notches, then Bill gave her half regulator, since he couldn't get any more. Then we began to fly, roaring through the two Moreton bridges like the 'Bristolian', and she rode like the coaches behind, straight and true, no dancing, jumping, or swaying, the red needle on the steam pressure gauge rock steady at 200lb, just, but not quite, at the blowing off stage.

I was enjoying myself now, this was a locomotive to appreciate, and I wished that they were all in this condition, what a pleasure it would be to come to work. Leaving Cholsey, Bill was able to link her up himself as the extra oil reached her valves, then he adjusted the lubricator feed, cutting back the supply a little, and by the time we reached Reading she was much easier, and she was steaming so well I was able to allow her fire to go, in fact when we arrived at Paddington her firebox was down to the extent that I could see the fire bars.

The return trip with the 7.40p.m. was just as enjoyable, it was one of those trips, few and far between, where everything goes so perfectly it was a shame to come to the end of the duty, all that I could wish for now was to have the same engine tomorrow, my last ever trip as a Great Western fireman (there would be the odd occasion, all unofficial, but not as a registered fireman). When I booked off, there was a message for me, I was requested to come on duty the next day and report to the District Inspector's office on number five platform before coming to the shed. I wondered what this was all about, well, tomorrow would see.

Somewhere in the passing-on process the message had got a bit altered, for I found the District Inspector's office was on number four platform, but told myself to knock at the door and go in, as he probably wanted to welcome me into the Traffic Department and there was nothing to worry about. A gruff voice bade me to enter, and I walked in to be confronted by District Inspector Stacey, a big bluff man with a heavy white moustache, wearing Inspector's uniform with a peaked cap loaded round the edge with black braid. So, this was the big boss man in charge of all the signalmen and boxes in the district. I stood there, all dressed up to do battle with a locomotive in an hour's time, my 'Grimsby' box in my hand, and he just sat there, clean, smart, the very last word in authority, eyeing me up and down. He made me bridle with his remark as to why I should think that I was good enough to be considered as a budding signalman (the old rivalry between Traffic and Locomotive Departments again!), but before I could think of a suitable answer he asked me to sit down, as he could see that my feathers were ruffled.

The questions began; how long had I been a railway man, did I think a signalman's life was an easy one, what was it that made me dissatisfied with engine work, why did I want to be a signalman? To that last one I gave him an answer that seemed to please him, for I told him that I thought that to be a signalman was one of the most rewarding jobs on the railway, and after that I thought the interview was over, but as I made ready to go, he motioned me to remain seated. Then the serious business began, as Tom Stacey began to put me through the rule book as it applied to footplate work. For three-quarters of an hour I was bombarded with questions, each of which I answered as well as I could, then he got up and came round his desk, shook hands with me and welcomed me into the Department, with the passing remark that the Locomotive Department had provided the rough casting, and that his Department would put the polish on.

Tom gave me a letter addressed to a Mr. Blackhall in charge of the Signal School at Reading, a Free Pass valid for one month, and instructions to report there on Monday morning at 8.00a.m. So, I was over the first hurdle.

I made my way down the path to the shed and book on duty for the last time, my feelings a mixture of sadness and elation, as I realised that this was the last locomotive to prepare, the last time off shed, and each time I picked up the shovel or put on the injector it was with a new perception. We had our new engine again, 6973, a fitting end to what I had once thought would be a career. When we ran in to Paddington and those big buffers loomed towards me for the last time, everything seemed to move at twice the speed as if the day and this final duty was in a hurry to be rid of me.

I enjoyed the run home, savouring every second, with no doubt in my mind now, just implanting in my memory the joys of loco-motive work; Bill hammered away and I shovelled the coal in, knowing that I was soaking it all in to be stored away for another day, the experience of working on steam locomotives that could never be taken away.

When I climbed down from the footplate for the last time it was with a very deep feeling of regret. I handed in my overalls, even the pair I was wearing, with just a sideways glance at our engine on the ash road; I had burnt my bridges, it was all part of the past, tomorrow was Sunday, a day off, and Monday would bring another battle.

Chapter Two

Back to School

Monday morning found me boarding the 7.05 a.m. from Didcot, on a bitter cold day with snow on the ground. I was going to work, for the first time in many years, without overalls, and I even had a white shirt on. It was with a bit of a smirk on my face that I looked towards the engine, 5935 *Norton Hall* back in service from her boiler washout, but someone else could shovel her to Paddington from now on. I heard her blow off running into Pangbourne, and I gave a sniff of disdain, but told myself 'forget it boyo, that is behind you now'. I walked down the platform at Reading without looking back, the sound of *Norton Hall* marching out keeping step with me, then round the corner towards where I thought this Signal School ought to be.

I went through a gateway and into a yard full of every kind of signal imaginable: gantries, homes, distants, starters, all laid down: there were piles of pulleys, coils of signal wire, and loose semaphore arms, and at the far end of the yard was a low blue brick building with a slate roof and four small dingy windows set back into the brickwork to allow room for the iron bars that protected the glass. It looked like a seedy run-down prison. There was one door into this building, painted in chocolate and cream about 1885 by the look of it, the paint being held in place by a cast iron plate which bore the words 'SIGNAL SCHOOL' and I think this was the most depressing place I had ever seen.

I knocked on the door and walked in, resplendent in my new footplate overcoat and jacket, both garments matching my flannels well. (Hand in all my uniform they had said last week, not likely, I wanted to have some railway uniform to start this job with just to show that I belonged, but it was to be my undoing in a moment.) Once inside I began to see that this building was something like a village hall, with a wooden floor, tables and chairs laid out in a row, and with an old friend in the middle, one of the cast iron stoves supplied in enginemen's cabins, the whole place soaked in an atmosphere of decay and damp, for even the fire was out after the Christmas break. Six low-powered bulbs, suspended through the length of the room, were on, so somebody had been in, but as far as I was aware I was the first of the students to arrive. At the end of the room was a sight that drew me like a magnet, a two-inch gauge model railway about fifteen feet in length, with a junction, cross-over, four running roads and a 0-6-0 tender engine sitting in the middle. The whole lot was fixed up with signals and wires connected to a miniature frame with block bells and instruments at either end, so thinking that the loco might be powered I made a move to pick it up, when a sharp voice told me to leave things alone, and I looked round in the dismal light to see a small man emerge from a cubby-hole in the corner, wearing an overcoat, scarf, and stained once-grey trilby hat. I had come into contact with Freddie Blackhall, Assistant District Inspector, and the Tutor of Reading Signalling School.

I gave him the letter and stood still as he walked round me, eyeing up and down my footplate overcoat, then he said five words, 'I don't like footplate men'. I kept my mouth shut, as it was quite obvious that I was the enemy. I had met drivers like him who didn't like firemen, in fact some of them didn't even seem to like themselves, so I waited and waited, until at last he read the letter which must have confirmed his worst fears, that I was indeed a footplate man, then he instructed me to exercise all my skill in getting the stove alight.

I scouted round that snow-covered yard for some wood, found a drum of signal oil propped up on a trestle, and a pile of loco coal. Within half an hour the rest of the budding signalmen trainees had arrived and Freddie was glad enough to take off his overcoat, because I had certainly exercised all my skill on the fire, and the mixture of wood blocks, signal oil and loco coal had that old stove roaring like a 'Castle'. That first day was spent learning the rudiments of signalling and block working, Freddie ignoring me completely, which I found hard as I was used to the warmth and comradeship of the footplate, but it was a case of sticking it out and seeing what transpired. Looking back now I can see that it was a wise decision, and the situation was to change, but that first day certainly seemed a long one.

We finished at 6.00p.m. which allowed plenty of time to catch the 6.30p.m. from Reading, so I returned home fairly elated, for with the dinner break of three-quarters of an hour it gave a working week of 46¼ hours, so I was gaining an hour and three-quarters in each week and going home clean.

Nowadays, with a working day from eight to five, with an hour for lunch and morning and afternoon tea breaks, those old conditions seem ludicrous, yet at the time the new arrangement seemed wonderful to me, for there had been no set meal breaks or hours on the footplate. Tuesday came and the tension eased a little, Wednesday morning Freddie greeted me when I came in, Thursday was even better, he called me by my first name, but Friday was to clear the air once and for all. When we arrived that morning Freddie had been busy, all our places had been set out with paper and pencil, for us to sit a simple examination. I wrote for an hour, answering each set question, then I laid down the pencil and sat back, while all around me a lot of whispering and pencil-chewing was going on. Freddie peered over the top of his glasses at me, and beckoned me to bring my papers to him, which I did and then returned to my desk. He began to read, going over each paper for a long time, until the rest of the lads had finished and it was time for the dinner break, and naturally the discussion between all of us was how we had answered those questions.

The rest of the afternoon was back to rules and regulations, not a word as to how this examination had gone, then when it was time to leave Freddie asked me to wait for him as he was coming with me. Not a word was spoken as we walked to the station, but I waited for him to make the first move. Freddie was obviously pondering something that had him beat, and as we pulled away from Reading he told me that I had answered every question in that examination correctly, but how *could* an ex-footplate man acquire such a knowledge of the basics of signal box work? As he questioned me, he found that I had become so enthusiastic about this type of railway work that I had spent every minute I could spare over the last nine months in signal boxes. Of course he wanted to know which boxes, so I told him, then which signalmen, but he had to grin when I wouldn't tell him that, and said that no way was I going to land those chaps who had helped me in trouble for having an unauthorised person in the box. This last statement was appreciated by him, and he held his hand out and admitted that he had weighed me up all wrong and that he had started off on the wrong foot, and from that moment on, Freddie and I became friends. He told me that the course was a three month one, with visits to signal boxes playing an important part of the last month.

The second week fairly flew by. Freddie would set out the work and as soon as I had finished he would come and sit by my side pointing out various small slips until the other lads had finished. In the evenings on the train going home he would talk about incidents during his time as a signalman, and how he had dealt with various situations, and now he was passing on all his knowledge on to me.

During the third week things really began to happen. Freddie took me into his little office and put me through a mock oral examination such as a regular signalman would take each year. He must have been satisfied because he called me in again on the Thursday, and told me that he could teach me no more, and that I was to report to District Inspector Checkley on Monday morning.

The real surprise came with the next bit of information, that there were two vacancies, one at Kingsworthy on the Winchester branch which was a Class Five box, and one at Milton on the main line which was a Class Three box. I could reasonably expect to be successful with my application for the Kingsworthy job, which would mean lodging, or a fast ninety-minute run each way on my AJS motorcycle. I had found out from experience, that faint heart never won fair lady, and so I applied for both vacancies, with Milton as first choice.

Sunday was a day off, and I put the rule book to one side, being full up to the brim with it in any case. I collected my young lady from the Great Western Hostel where she worked and lived-in, and took her for a morning walk. The snow had gone, leaving everything wet and muddy although it was still bitterly cold. We walked for a couple of miles enjoying each other's company, my hands turning blue, not with cold, but from the dye in the woollen gloves which my young lady was wearing — ah, the passion of youth! When I took her back to the Hostel she informed me that I would not be seeing her any more that day as she had to wash her hair, a ritual all ladies go through which seems to last for hours.

Sunday afternoon in Didcot was scarcely a riot of activity. I could look at the ten shops, wish it was seven in the evening when the Coronet cinema opened, or I could get on the bike and go for a spin. There happened to be a motor cycle trial on at Aldsworth on top of the Berkshire Downs, so I set off to see if I could learn a few tips from the experts. They had 'observed sections', a familiar word, as I had been bashing 'sections' into my head for the last few weeks, but these sections were a little different, great patches of mud, around big rocks, and up banks of one in one. I stood at one mud patch and watched the Six Day Internationals go through. Fred Rist, on a BSA was first, straight through and no messing, then came Alan Jefferies, roaring through, with mud flying everywhere. My hero, Hugh Viney, was next, riding an AJS like the one I owned, so I positioned myself behind the section to watch his line through. He came along, lined up to a tree the other side of the section, the big single cylinder engine turning over with a slow steady 'plonk plonk' then he was through and away. There seemed nothing to it, it was just like taking a 'twenty-eight' up a bank, and after all I could do that. After the last rider had gone through, the Section Marshall allowed me to have a go. I lined up with that tree, put the bike in second gear, and in I went, 'plonk plonk' just the same as the expert, only I hit a rock in the middle that didn't seem to be there when *he* went through. The laughter from the spectators was genuine as they lifted the bike off me, and I rode home covered in mud, my beautiful black gleaming bike now a sorry mess, thinking, everyone to his own trade. It took me months to clean it all off, but, for a few hours my mind had been clear of block bells and signals.

Monday morning came, and I set off for the interview with Bill Checkley. I had never met him, but not many of the lads had, because during the three weeks that I had been at Reading, Tom Stacey had retired and Bill Checkley had taken over. When I first met him that morning, I didn't quite know what to make of him. He was a big, tall smart man, ex-Household Cavalry, still with the spit and polish about him. His bearing was very cold and clinical, and he came out with probing questions as one would expect from a police inspector. Freddie must have briefed him about me, because he made no attempt to question me on the rules and regulations. He told me to report to Milton signal box under instruction, until he contacted me again, but he did emphasise strongly, that this did not have anything to do with my application for the vacancy at that box. I thanked him and left, and later when I got to know him better I found that he was a great chap, his hobby was growing roses and he was good enough at it for him to be an acknowledged expert.

Although I was told that this move was nothing to do with my application, I naturally had hopes, and there was one part of the overall picture that was in my favour, for no one had ever gone through the school at Reading in only three weeks, and certainly no one had started in a Class Three main line box. Now I had accomplished the first part, I would go all out to finish the second half, telling myself that there was a first time for everything. I would pull out all the stops, and if I didn't make it, it wouldn't be for want of trying.

I rode my bike down the footpath towards Foxhall Junction Signal Box, and as I drew near to the box, Bill Ackrill slid the rear window open, and wished me all the luck in the world. I had gone to school with both his sons, Frank and Bill. Frank had made a career in local council work, but Bill had come up through the ranks of engine cleaning and firing with me, and he was one of those who had left the service for a better job. So Bill in the signal box knew first hand of the change that I had made. The conversation was mostly leg-pulling, but Bill was pleased that I had managed this transfer, and, that I was going to be at Milton. He pointed out one thing that I had not even thought about. Bill Checkley must have briefed the signalman at Milton and a report of my progress would be required every week, which was more food for thought on my part.

I cycled on down the path which ran alongside the Up loop. This was familiar ground since I had spent hours in this same loop during the last winter, in charge of six freight trains blocked back by Control. Keeping the fires and boilers up on the six locomotives had been like painting the Forth Bridge, as by the time I had dealt with each one and worked my way back, it was time to start all over again.

As I cycled round the gentle sweep of the curve past Foxhall Down Main advanced starter signal, Milton Box came into view, a box that I had passed many times on the footplate taking little notice. It had been built in 1942 to replace the old wooden box that was situated on the Steventon side of the road bridge, and it was exactly half way between Steventon station and Foxhall Junction. In construction it was a standard box, as was to be found all over the system, built of red brick with a flat concrete roof.

I had no idea who would be on duty, but as I approached, the end window was pushed open, and it was with relief and pleasure that I saw Bert Vokings beaming down at me, a chap I had known for years. I placed my bike beneath the box and climbed the stairs to meet him. He had a cup of tea waiting, and he held his hand out to greet me. This was the kind of welcome that I was used to; the footplate kind. I decided that the Traffic Department lads were not so bad after all, and now that I had joined them, I was fully accepted.

From that moment onwards, Bert took me under his wing and gave me every encouragement and help that it was possible to give. So much so, that in similar circumstances, where I had been in the position to help somebody, I was always reminded of Bert Vokings, and did my best to uphold the old Great Western tradition and help give a 'leg over the stile' to someone in need.

Bert sounded me out, learning all about my visits to other boxes, and the progress that I had made at Reading. He explained every detail of the workings of the box to me, and I just sat and watched him operate the box, gradually taking in all the procedures. On Tuesday morning I was up early, and back at Milton at 6.00a.m. to start the shift with Bert. I began a type of sound practical training that was to prove invaluable. Milton box was equipped with 38 levers covering the Up and Down goods loops, each with a lead in and out, the Up and Down main lines, and a cross-over. The box dealt with an average of sixty trains each shift, and during the eight-hour duty, the block was always occupied, and I decided that perhaps it was a good thing after all that I had been sent to Milton, instead of a small country box with one train each hour, as it altered my perception, and I became used to dealing with heavy traffic as normal working practice.

Bert's training began by allowing me to take care of all the Down traffic for the first few days, then I dealt with all of the Up traffic, whilst he took care of the telephones and bookings. This first early turn was made easy by the chaps in the signal boxes on both sides of me; Bill Ackrill at Foxhall Junction and Arthur Stoner at Steventon. They had both been warned that a novice was in the box between them.

Bell signals are laid down in the regulations as distinct sounds. A goods train was coded as 3—4—1 with a pause between each beat on the block bell. I therefore sent the codes in this manner, and received the reply in a similar manner. Under normal practice, however, that would have been sent as eight bells, rattled out as quickly as the signalman could operate the key, and I soon learned how to work this way. It was surprising how, in later years, I could always tell if a Relief man was either side of me, as each man had his own distinctive way of operating the key. It was instantly known when the regular man was missing. I completed that first week, confident that I was making good progress, and then the following week introduced me to my first period of night duty from 10.00p.m. to 6.00a.m. I soon found that the track circuits, signal repeaters, and the illuminated diagram were essential for night working, but, by the end of the week, Bert was allowing me to work both Up and Down traffic whilst he sat back and passed on advice.

On Sunday morning we banked up the fire and switched the box out, which was a simple matter providing that the block instruments read the same, either 'line clear' or 'train on line'. We sent the bell signal to indicate switching out to the two boxes on either side of us and went home, ready to return at 2.00p.m.

On our return, we telephoned the boxes on either side to see what was on the block, and then we switched back in. We were now back in business again until 10.00 p.m. On that Sunday, traffic was quiet, so Bert took the opportunity of going through the rules with me, which he did regularly, and after eight hours I went home feeling tired out. I began to wonder if it had been worthwhile. Footplate work had been tiring enough, but with all that I had crammed in during this last four weeks, I was dead-beat.

On Monday afternoon, I was back at 2.00 p.m. ready to start the late turn, and Bert sat back watching me operate the box, since I was now able to cope with the booking and the telephone. Bert was always there in case I got into a tangle. I was unaware what he was reporting back to Bill Checkley, and was far too busy even to think about it. What I did not know was that Bert was making certain plans, which was perhaps just as well, if I had known, I would have flunked out with sheer fright.

I realised on that Monday afternoon that I could deal with up to six trains, glancing at the clock for the times, booking it all in the register when the busy period was over, so I must have been making progress. At nine in the evening, I found to my surprise, that I had dealt with everything; signals, booking and telephones, and made decisions on routing trains either up the loops or turning out onto the main line without once having to confirm with Bert. I went home tired; as tired as ever I had gone home from the footplate, the physical effort not being far short of shovelling. In addition there had been the mental concentration, but I went home happy as well as tired, as a little bit of satisfaction was beginning to sink in.

Tuesday came, and with it, Bert's well-laid plans. We had a cup of tea, and at about three in the afternoon he casually mentioned that he was going to check on the coal bunker. I knew that we were getting low, and I had made arrangements with the driver of the 'Up Fly' to drop off a couple of tons later on, but Bert was insistent that he had to have a look. I thought nothing of it at the time, and carried on with the work. First I dealt with an Up freight, and then pulled off the signals for a Down fast, and it was only when my advanced starting signal came off in the distance that I saw a small figure on a bike disappearing under Steventon road bridge. Was it Bert? It certainly looked like him, so I clattered down the stairs and found that the coal bunker was still there, but no Bert! He had obviously sent me solo!

Since that time I have always had the utmost sympathy with the trainee aeroplane pilot who is going solo for the first time. I began to imagine that every kind of emergency was going to happen, but the trains went by, I booked them in, dealt with others, and in between prayed that Bert would return soon.

A 'twenty-eight' stuck her nose under the bridge, turned her front end into the loop, her long rake of wagons snaking behind her, and as she passed under the window, I could hear the slap, slap, of her vacuum pump, and the usual shouted remarks about wire netting roofs. It was now my turn to give the sign of two fingers up in the air, for the wheel had turned full circle.

Bert rang me up from Steventon a couple of hours later to say that he was on the way back and would I please put the kettle on. He came up those stairs with a funny grin on his face. He knew as well as I did, that I had coped all right and in those few hours, I had aged a few years and become a signalman in the process.

This pattern was repeated for the next couple of days, Bert riding over to Foxhall on Wednesday, and to Steventon again on Thursday, leaving me for longer periods each time, but on Friday afternoon he stayed at Milton, so perhaps something was in the wind. The wind, in this instance, took the shape of District Inspector Bill Checkley cycling towards us, but we had received prior warning, by telephone, from Bill Ackrill at Foxhall, and I am sure that Bert already had an idea that this visit might come off.

Bill Checkley sat in his chair and watched, and I found it very unnerving to be under his scrutiny, but I carried on putting into practice what Bert had hammered into me. Bill asked me a few simple questions on the rules, then at four o'clock he made a move, with the parting remark that, on Monday morning, I was to report to Chief Inspector Honeybone at Paddington for my final examination. Bert was jubilant at this news, which made it look as if I might, after all, get the appointment at Milton; this would then allow him to achieve his ambition of moving on to Didcot West End, as the only thing holding him back was someone to replace him at Milton.

In the few short weeks I had been in the Traffic Department, I had heard the name of Chief Inspector Honeybone referred to many times, he was a gentleman who had the reputation of being a 'holy terror', sending signalmen back for further training at an alarming rate. He was reputed to be rough, tough, and the ultimate expert on all signalling matters, and he expected those who came up before him to be on the top line. I managed to get through the Saturday somehow, with Bert coaching me, trying all the rules and incidents he could think of, and I managed to find answers to most of them, and I found out that Mister Honeybone was all that he was reputed to be. When Monday morning came, I walked down to the station with a quaking heart, collected my free pass from the Booking Office, and caught the familiar 7.05 a.m. up from Didcot. It didn't seem possible that six short weeks ago I could have been working this train on the footplate, and yet now, here I was with three weeks of signalling school behind me and three weeks of signal box training under my hat, going to Paddington to meet this terrible man.

The old well-remembered landmarks slipped past, the biscuits at Reading with the pot-bellied little fireless locomotive puffing out from the dark confines of the factory, and at Slough, the tang of Horlicks, Mars bars and Exlax (not that I needed any of that, the very thought of this meeting had seen me in the toilet enough times). When I arrived at Paddington I was in a real state, wound up tight and feeling sick. It was a period of exquisite torture indeed, and I still get the same feeling before going to do a talk to various railway clubs.

I stopped to have a word with my old mates on the footplate of 6923 *Croxteth Hall* simmering quietly after her run. As I swung up onto the footplate and sat down on the fireman's seat, I watched my friend Roy Saunders pull some coal forward. At that moment I would have given anything to change places with him. His driver, Roy Frewin, gave me a cup of tea out of the can, and I had a cigarette. *Croxteth Hall* began to simmer at the safety valve, so with a nod from Roy, I put on the live steam injector, and that simple act took some of the tension out of me. I still knew how to handle a boiler, but all too soon the pilot engine pulled the coaches away, and I had to leave the footplate.

I walked over the 'Green' and up the stairs towards the offices. I knew Paddington well, but not this part, and, feeling like a condemned man, I went down a dingy passage, turned a corner into a highly polished corridor and knocked on a heavy oak door thinking that, somewhere, there must be someone who could tell me where to go. There was no answer to my knocking, so I turned the big brass knob and walked into a room that looked like the Number One Court of the Old Bailey, with oak panelling all round the walls. I saw a gigantic oak table, running almost the entire length of the room, its surface polished like glass, and heavy oak chairs spaced all round, not an inch out of place. The oil paintings on the wall were also spaced out with precision.

I walked round this room looking back into the eyes of Gooch, Armstrong, Dean, Churchward, as they stared at me from their portraits; they were all there, the great men of the Western, but I remember that Sir Felix Pole did not look amused. It was obvious to me that I had walked into the Great Western Boardroom, so I thought that while I was here, I might just as well have a good look around, since I had a quarter of an hour to spare. On the big sideboard at the far end of the room I could see a model of a 'King' locomotive inside a glass case, but I never got that far, as there was a half-strangled screech behind me, and I turned round to be confronted by a stout little man dressed in a uniform which looked like that of an Admiral of the Fleet, but without the cap. He was most upset and wanted to know who I was, where did I come from, what was I doing in here, and so forth. I then noticed a little word embroidered on his collar, it was 'Messenger', so I realised that there was no need to call him 'Sir', and he wasn't a railwayman. It took me five minutes to quieten this excitable little man down and get him to address *me* as 'Sir'. After all, I did have my best suit on, and I had explained my presence and where I wanted to go. On the way out he breathed on that big brass door knob and gave it a polish with his handkerchief, as if I had con-taminated this inner sanctum of power. He then took me along other corridors until we came to a door marked 'Chief Inspector', and I had arrived. I knocked on the door, and walked in to find myself inside a small room with a bench down the length of one side, and a door to an adjoining office leading off. The bench was full of pale, twitching nervous lads, all cramming out of the red signal book, just like a Swindon examination room, and I joined them on the bench after a shuffle-up to make room for me.

From inside the other office we could hear murmurings, followed by shouting, then the door opened and a lad crept out, his face burning with shame. A voice barked 'Next', and the lad at the end of the row went in. There was more shouting, and out he came, and so it went on until I was left on my own. I was welded to that bench, my toes digging into my shoes, my fingers gripping underneath the padded seat, waiting for that shout, and when it came I would be out of the door and down the platform as fast as I could go. I waited and waited, and gradually began to relax, until I was on the point of chancing a cigarette when the office door opened, and a quiet voice bade me enter. Perhaps the Good Lord had taken pity on me and Chief 'Executioner' Honeybone had gone out of another door and that this gentleman was the kind one. When I had a good look at him I saw that he was the one, sure enough. He sat there behind his desk, a small man, slightly built, stern looking and cold, with his cap and its gold-leafed brim set square on his head, peering at me over the top of his spectacles, and if he had put on a wig and gown, he would have assumed the proportions of a High Court Judge.

He studied the papers before him, and commented on the fact that I was an ex-footplate man. So he had my records, but there was nothing in that to be worried about, as I had never been late, ill, or in any scrapes — none that they could prove anyway. Then the inquisition began, and to my surprise it was on footplate rules, put in a gentle manner and I began to unwind. He then turned to the signalling rules; first the emergencies, these he expected to be answered correctly and without hesitation, because if such an emergency occurred, the reaction of the signalman had to be instant — there would be no time to fumble through a book of rules to see what had to be done.

I got through these without any trouble, because thanks to the coaching by Freddie Blackhall and Bert Vokings, and to my own study of the regulations, I knew them off by heart. Indeed, I still do, twenty-two years afterwards, they were like the multiplication tables at school, once hammered in they were there forever!

The complicated questions came next, dealing with those situations which make one think before answering. The odd sneaky one was thrown in for good measure, such as: what would I do if the platelayer came stumbling through a thick pea-soup fog to tell me that the wind had just blown down a large tree across the main line? I thought about that for one a minute, and then I replied, somewhat flippantly, that I would get him to jack up the tree while I shovelled the fog under it, just enough to lift it higher than a locomotive!

He took off his Chief Inspector's hat at that one, and tried a question on single line working: what would I do if I had two trains on the same line in the section? I told him that I would resign. Mr. Honeybone gave me a smile, looked at his watch and said that he had heard enough. He came round from behind his desk, placed his hands on my shoulders, and told me that he had heard all about me from Freddie Blackhall. Bless dear old Freddie, I thought, he had opened the door for me after all. As I was thinking this, Mr. Honeybone gave me the biggest surprise of all, when he said that, providing Bill Checkley, my District Inspector, agreed, there was no reason why I should not fill the vacancy at Milton.

22

I shook hands with him and went out of that office elated to the extent that I hardly knew what day it was. All the tension drained away to be replaced by such happiness that I was in a state of euphoria such as I had never known. After all, in six weeks, I had gone from a fireman's job to a Class Three main line appointment. All that I had heard about this man was untrue, and although our paths were to cross again many times, I always found him to be a gentleman. I walked out of Paddington, up Praed Street and into a pub for a couple of pints: I'm not normally a drinking man, but I reckoned that I had earned those. I still remember those two pints, and, at the risk of offending the lads 'up the Smoke' I must say it was some wishy-washy stuff, not a man's drink at all. I can remember even after all these years, wondering how they could fire a 'King' on such stuff!

When I got back to Didcot, I made my way to the office to report, and as I walked in, Freddie Blackhall bounded round the desk and shook my hand, as he had heard the result by telephone. I was delighted to see him, and to hear that he had finished with the Reading Signal School and was now working the district as assistant to Bill Checkley. Bill was out at the moment, so Freddie told me to carry on at Milton for the rest of the week, then he gave me a wink and a playful punch on the arm and told me to get off home. My 'old chap' was delighted to hear my news. While I had been training, I had been down on porter's money, but with this new rating, I would be up to a fireman's wage again, plus the added bonus of regular night-shift pay, and one Sunday in three at that special rate of pay. It was still not a lot of course, because railway pay was never as good as that paid in the factories, but it was enough to make me think of a settled future and to allow me to ensnare a certain young lady before someone else beat me to it. After all, I could hope for promotion once I had got to grips with this new job.

When I returned to Milton the next morning, I found that the 'jungle telegraph' had worked in the Traffic Department just the same as on the locomotive side. Bert's pleasure was beyond bounds, as all the hard work he had devoted to me had paid off. All that morning the phones rang with congratulations, and one call came from Bill Ackrill at Foxhall, warning that Bill Checkley was on his way. Cups, saucers, teapot, and most importantly, the forbidden portable radio were hidden away so that when he arrived, the box would be the picture of decorum. Bill came into sight, a small figure pedalling away far up the line, and as he came near we could see that he was going to miss the small wooden bridge over the point rodding, as he was too busy looking into the goings-on in the Army Depot at the other side of the fence. There was nothing to see really, just a lot of old wheel barrows, and when Bill picked himself up, we were looking the other way, as we had no wish to let him see us laughing, because this was the moment of truth for me, the final test had come. Bill came up into the box breathing hard, and with a cut on his hand, which we bound up for him: sooner or later he would let on what had given him so much interest in that depot. He sat there watching me work the box for an hour, and then he told me that I could take over on the night shift the following week, and that Bert could go to Didcot West End and begin to learn that box. The next step was to get Bert to sign the form, the form which became a statement, that in the opinion of the signalman handing over I was fully competent to discharge my duties correctly at Milton. Bert signed, and was pleased to do so, a duty which I found pleasing when signing the form for other lads.

Bill shook hands with me, and a frosty smile crept over his face; those stony features took on a new dimension with that smile, but looking back, I can now see why Bill had been so wary to begin with. He had just taken over the district, his first, so he had been feeling his way and, then, just as he thought that everything was perfect, this ex-footplate man had come roaring through. He had every right to feel a bit uncertain about me, for in those six short weeks I had broken through all known procedure, but I made a promise to Bill that I would never break, I would not in any way let him down.

I cycled up the path towards Foxhall with Bert that last Saturday afternoon, knowing that the next time I came this way it would be to take over. I had a long weekend ahead of me, which came round regularly, and was looked forward to by every signalman because one did not have to return to duty until 10.00 p.m. on the Monday night. I was at a loose end. My darling Betty had gone home to Wales on the first of many forays which young ladies make once a wedding date is fixed. (The wedding was not until August, but already in mid-February the ground-work had begun.) That Saturday afternoon I was very preoccupied with my thoughts about the responsibilities of the coming Monday night. My old Dad could see this, and with the typical ease of a father understanding his son better than he did himself, he knew that I would be all right once I had got over that first night, but until then I needed to be taken out of myself, and given something different to do and to think about, which Dad set out to achieve.

The first step was to get me to go down with him to the Staff Association Club that evening, for a couple of pints and a game of darts. We were both good players, and a near miss on a double was just not tolerated. There would be gentle jibes such as 'amateur' and 'you're supposed to hit the double not the wire' or considerably stronger comments passing between us, but we were pretty evenly matched, and the remarks were all in good fun and certainly helped to take my mind off my worries. After the game we sat down to enjoy our drink, and then Dad leaned over and touched me on the knee, and in his crafty way, came out with a remark which he knew would make me rise to the bait he had prepared in his mind. Now that I was occupied with a job in a 'greenhouse' with a table and chair, a toilet, regular hours and even wearing a white shirt, just like the gentry, perhaps I considered myself just a little bit superior, and perhaps my hands had got too soft to handle a shovel?

My 'old chap' had a way of being deadly serious when he was pulling my leg, and every time he tried it I got caught, this time included. I replied rather indignantly, that my hands might be clean, but they were not soft, and I was every bit as skilled with the shovel as he had ever been, and I could fire any type of locomotive he cared to put in front of me, whereas he had been a driver for so many years that he was beginning to lose touch with firing. The conversation was going just the way he had intended: 'Right' he said, 'if you're so good you can come with me tomorrow, to give my fireman a rest. We've got a nice little run to Eastleigh with a farm special'.

I must have been made to fall for it, but it happened that a farm special was one type of train that I had never worked on during my firing days. This one would be coming through from Yorkshire, consisting of the farm machinery and household goods, while the cattle would be following by another special later in the day.

Father was due off shed at 9.00 a.m. that Sunday morning, so I arranged to be on the platform soon after then, thinking that there was no point in letting the Foreman know what was going on by going into the shed myself, although he probably would not have minded anyway. I climbed the steps to the platform, my footsteps sounding hollow on this quiet morning, and found the farm special standing alongside number five platform. It was quite a sizeable train, with a dozen flats loaded with reapers, binders, ploughs, tractors and various odds and ends, and then came two containers and finally a third brake coach with the family and employees aboard.

As I got to the end of the platform I looked back towards the engine shed, expecting to see a 'Grange' or a 'Mogul' poking her nose out, since father had assured me that a good engine was booked for this job, but then I found he had delivered a blow right under the belt as he came sliding quietly up to the shed signal with the little Didcot Dean Goods No. 2573. Poor little old lady, she had been built back in the eighties, with a boiler pressure of only 180lb., and now with the flap of her spindle glands pegged up over the front buffer she looked as if she was grinning at me, just like the 'old chap' was, as she chuffed up over the points and then set back on to the train. My hands were clean at the moment, but it looked as if I would be getting them dirty in a few minutes, so I might just as well start now, and tie her on. I slipped down between the platform and the tender and coupled her up, then climbed up onto the footplate, looking deadly serious, and not allowing either my father or his fireman any satisfaction in their smirking.

Tom, the fireman, climbed down and went back to install himself in the coach with the Sunday newspapers, being only too pleased to spend the next couple of hours relaxing on a comfortable seat. I hung up my jacket, took off my tie and rolled up my sleeves, determined to show the senior member of the family that I had not forgotten my old craft in a few short weeks. The timing of this train was so easy that it would be a doddle in any case. We had an hour to get to Newbury, another hour to Winchester, then half an hour to Eastleigh. Her fire was burning through nicely, so I packed some coal in the back corners of the firebox, which would last until we were on the branch. The guard blew his whistle, father placed the reverser in full fore gear, opened the little push-over regulator two inches off the guide stop, and we were away, drifting over the junction, round the curve and onto the branch.

As soon as she began to tilt her nose up, he linked her back with the pole reverser, and gave her half a regulator and left her there, letting her set her own pace. I fed the fire, in the back corners, front corners, round the sides of the box, and then a couple of shovelfuls sprayed into the middle, each shovelful of coal tingeing her exhaust with a slight brown stain. Half a mile further on, I went round the box again, sliding the underneath of the shovel on the fire hole ring, angling it round until the fire took on the shape of a big saucer. This was really expert firing, turning the fire into a sculpture, just as William Dean had designed the firebox to accept! The 'old chap' had a look inside, sniffed, then knocked his pipe out on my newly swept floorboards, but even if father was pretending to be unimpressed with my fire, the little engine loved it, and began to sing as the steam pressure needle hovered on the 180 lb. red line. Her old flower pot safety valve perched high on top of the boiler just ahead of the two small cab windows, began to lift, and there was a soft mellow whisper of steam, as if she was purring with contentment as the white flower of steam drifted back over the tiny cab roof. I opened the tender water feed and turned the wire wheel of the right hand live steam injector two turns, then I tapped back the water feed until the overflow was gone, and the injector settled down to a quiet singing, as she drank gently from her water supply. I turned on the coal watering pipe and hosed down the pipe ash and a pair of shining boots, the water in the gauge glass bobbing up and down, each rise a little higher up the glass than the last, and when it reached three-quarters full, she had lost twenty pounds of steam pressure, so it was time to shut the injector off for another mile or so.

It was a pleasure to be back, to feel the pulse of this little engine as she lifted the train up the bank towards Upton, and I realised that I had missed the warmth of the cab, the aroma of hot oil, steam and the whiff of good Welsh coal burning as the smoke rolled back from the chimney. Looking over the side I could see her small side rods going up and over, and hear her little heart beating, 'chuff, chuff, chuff, chuff' four little beats out of the chimney for each revolution of her driving wheels, her stubby boiler sniffing out the line ahead, lining up to go through Upton station bridge.

I began to fire her again round the box, dropping and lifting the flap between each shovelful. As she tackled the bank, the lever was dropped forward a couple of notches and her exhaust deepened, the tall chalk walls of the cutting throwing back the echo, and the lineside rabbits began to run, tumbling over in their haste to escape, or scampering up the sheer cliffs, scrabbling their way up to the accompaniment of a miniature avalanche of chalk rubble. The cutting began to drop away and we were clearing the top, out over the beautiful rolling Berkshire Downs, the reverser was linked back and the regulator eased down. I dropped the firebox flap and put the injector on again as we rolled through Churn Halt, then down through Compton with a cheery wave to the signalman, down the dip at a rush, putting a little steam into her cylinders to Hampstead Norris. Next came the long climb up through the trees to Hermitage, her little chimney barking away until we shut off going through Pinewood Halt, and rolled down to Newbury with the wheel flanges squealing as they bit into the sharp curve on the approach to Newbury East Junction. Up the middle road we went, and stopped at Newbury West to fill the tank at the water-column; I clambered over the coal to lift the flap and catch the chain as the column was pulled round, and just then I could see Jessie Barnett, the Newbury Relief signalman coming down the box steps with two empty coal buckets. Now Jessie was quite a character, a stout bluff ruddy-faced man, bubbling over with good nature and fun. He didn't ask the fireman to fill his buckets, up on the footplate he came and helped himself, pulling my leg about firing to father. It was the 'old chap' who let the cat out of the bag, by telling Jessie not only that I had become a signalman, but also that I was off duty and doing this turn just for the fun of it. Jessie began to laugh, and he was still at it when we pulled away, and I saw him lifting the telephone ear piece, the news was evidently going ahead of us.

We chuffed along gently down the Berks and Hants main line, then swung onto the Winchester branch, passing Enbourne Junction where we caught sight of Dare Warwick, the signalman, leaning out of the box window holding up his coal shovel in one hand and the red signalman's book in the other, which was all that he could think of by way of a joke in the short time that he had. We pulled strongly up the bank to Woodhay where we joined the single line, thinking it curious that there was no sign of a signalman, but when I collected the token from the carrier the steel hoop handle was covered in wet red paint, which showed that the vendetta was beginning.

At Highclere, I dropped the Woodhay token on the platform and with the ease of one who had exchanged tokens before, I collected the Burghclere one from the outstretched arm, only to find the hoop covered with wet tea leaves! Down the dip, through the bridge and round the corner into Litchfield, where the exchange was made, apparently without a hitch, until I realised as I hung the new token on the hook in the cab, that this one was smeared with sticky condensed milk. My old Dad had a lot to answer for, but he just sat there, arms folded, sucking away at his awful pipe, grinning wider and wider as we progressed south.

As we ambled down the bank into Whitchurch, I was sitting on the seat removing the remains of paint, tea leaves and condensed milk from my hands, with some paraffin-soaked cotton waste. I was reckoning on being safe at Whitchurch, because there was a lady signalwoman there who exchanged tokens by the rule book, the old token being hung on the catcher and the new one being taken out of the rack. Father was giving our little engine a whiff on the vacuum brake, just enough to slow her down a little, but still fast enough to give my hand a healthy smack as I picked up the token. A little steam was put into her cylinders now, and I began to fire her gently for the climb out of Sutton Scotney and over the top. We rolled down into Worthy Down, the lovely Hampshire Downs looking wonderfully soft in the sunshine, and it was time to sit down and enjoy the view, with the regulator shut and flap down, as we coasted through Kingsworthy, through the tunnel and into Winchester.

We waited for ten minutes until the Southern T9 came up and clear with a train of empty coaches, then we were away again, over the long sweeping curve of Shawford Viaduct where we handed over the Southern token in its little leather pouch, and down the main line, enough steam being fed into her cylinders to keep her rolling into Eastleigh. On reaching our destination, I uncoupled, and we cleared the main line into the shed, while the Southern pilot engine collected our train and pulled it clear of the station and into the sidings. We turned on the triangle, then dropped back on to an empty shed road where the guard and the now well-rested fireman were waiting. It was agreed by all concerned, that I could still fire a Great Western steam locomotive, indeed, so good was I at it, and so skilled in boiling enough water to get us here, that the vote was passed that I should be able to make the tea without supervision.

While they were drinking their tea and chatting to the few Southern men who were about on this Sunday, I took the opportunity to have a look round, because to be let loose in a big Southern main line shed was too good a chance to miss, particularly as this was, in all probability, the last time I would ever be on Eastleigh shed. I had fired Southern engines, the 'Remembrance' class, and Urie's 'Moguls', and my feelings towards these locomotives was one of very happy memories, from the time when the Great Western had them on loan for about a year during the war to ease the engine shortage. Later, when the Swindon-built L.M.S. 84XX class came into service, together with the 'Austerity' class, we lost these fine engines, because the Southern naturally wanted them back, and I for one, was sorry to see them go.

As might be expected with a main line next to the Works, Eastleigh was similar to Swindon, there was plenty to see, and on a quiet Sunday, there was a chance to see it without getting in anyone's way. I had a good look round a 'Merchant Navy', and was surprised to look into that big square firebox after being used to the long narrow fireboxes of the Great Western. The 'King Arthur' class was big and powerful, everything that I had expected this locomotive to be, equal to one of our 'Kings' but it was a little bit disconcerting to find that the cab seemed so small after our Collett cabs. I could never have got used to that small Southern shovel, it was so heavy and narrow, without the fine balance of the Swindon product, but I suppose it depends on what one is used to.

There was one locomotive on the railway that I really did want to see, and to climb all over, and that was the 'Schools' class. In the end, I found one at the rear of the shed, tucked away in a line of other locomotives, and if she was in for repair, then she didn't look like it, because she shone brightly. Her home shed must have thought the world of her, and I was all over her, and underneath her, just looking and admiring. The slant of the inclined cab gave her a racy look. On the footplate she seemed to have plenty of room, all her cab fittings and copper pipe work gleamed, the reversing wheel had been burnished, and the boiler front paint-work reflected the long double regulator handle, painted deep red, the driver's end shut tight down on to the stop, the other end up in the roof. Out of all the locomotives that I had fired, this class had eluded me, and, it was the one class that I would have given anything to work on. Had she been in steam then I would have gone to find the Foreman, for even a trip round the triangle would have been better than nothing.

That was the last time that I saw a 'Schools', until thirty years later, when I was on a visit to the Bluebell Railway in East Sussex. One Sunday, as I turned the corner of the repair shop, there inside stood a 'Schools', 928 *Stowe*, looking just a little bit tatty after her many years outside. Perhaps one day before I become too feeble to lift a shovel, my Bluebell membership may allow me to see her in steam.

It was time to go home, our little Dean Goods looked ludicrous parked between those big Southern 'Merchant Navys', and so with the footplate filled now with two extra bodies (the fireman and the guard) we chuffed gently up to the shed signal. I operated the old indicator instrument which told the signalman where we wanted to go, the points came over, the ground signal clanged off and we were away. Up through the station, past Shawford Junction, until at Winchester Junction, it was over the fields on the new cut-off, back on to the branch and set sail for home.

For a day's work that was the result of a bit of kidding from my father, it had been worth every penny, figuratively speaking, because of course, I was not being paid for this, but I wouldn't have missed the trip for anything. It had completely taken my mind off my first duty in a signalbox, and proved that I could still handle the shovel, so all in all it had been a very satisfactory day.

Chapter Three

Playing my way in

Monday gradually passed, as I waited to go on that fateful duty at 10.00p.m. During the afternoon I went to bed for a couple of hours but I could not rest, and it was a relief when the clock said it was time to go. It was a beautiful evening as I cycled down the road towards Foxhall, the moonlight lighting up the old Provender Stores like the battlements of some border castle. Through the gate I went, and free wheeled down the path, over the crossing of West curve, with the lights of Foxhall Junction box casting a warm glow as I passed. I crossed the Up loop, then cycled along the path, the Down advanced starting signal with Milton's distant beneath it coming off just then as if to give me a clear line.

As I mounted the steps of Milton box, the 9.40p.m. Oxford parcels train came pounding down the main line working hard, building up speed from the West curve restriction. Jack Gardner, the late turn signalman, was pleased to see me, as we were old school mates from years back. We had a few words on the change-over, before Jack had to go, his cycle rear light bobbing as he crossed the wooden bridges over the point rodding. I was at last alone, ready to start my first ever duty in my own signal box. At 10.20p.m. the Up main block bell rang, making me nearly jump out of my skin, it was the Swindon parcels train, then the Down main block bell rang for the 8.55p.m. out of Paddington. I got 'line clear' from Foxhall and from Steventon and pulled off the signals: 28, 33, 34 and 35 for the Up train, 8, 3, 2 and 1 for the Down train. Now I was really in business, I thought, as both trains roared by, their tail lamps dancing as they passed, then it was 'Train out of section' on the bells, and signals back to normal, nothing to it, really, I told myself.

I had my two regular mates in the boxes each side of me, Arthur Stoner at Steventon and Bill Ackrill at Foxhall, two railway gentlemen, who treated this raw new man in the middle with every consideration, sending bell signals so slow and precise that even an idiot could have understood what was going on. I was to work with those two chaps for the next three years, and I found that the comradeship that existed on the footplate was also in the Traffic Department. A good example was with my first emergency that night, when a goods train came up with a hot axle box, and Arthur rang me up on the 'phone and told me that he was going to send me seven bells for 'stop and examine train', but to send it on to Foxhall as the train was running safely, and that the footplate chaps were aware of it.

Being helped in this way, I could hardly go wrong! Such close collaboration between signalmen was an essential part of signal box life, for although each train was the responsibility of the particular signalman whose block it was in, we could help one another out considerably with information and collaboration. This friendliness and dependence on each other was just like that between a driver and his fireman, so I soon began to feel at home.

They continued to treat me with care, but of course, as I progressed so did the work, and in a few weeks they were back to sending bell codes in the normal way, and I could receive and send as good as they could, 1–3–1, or 3–1–1, or 5 and 2–3 on the bells were all rattled out in one long string. In any case, now that I knew the service, I knew which bell codes to expect. The only change came with an emergency bell signal, and that was always sent in such a correct manner there was no doubt by the recipient as to what it meant.

That first night I dealt with 56 trains during the eight hour shift, seven per hour, which was pretty easy going, but as it took nine minutes for a passenger train to be on the block instruments from start to finish, and sixteen for a freight train, the block was always occupied. It was not all through traffic, however, some were turned out from the loop to the main line (which meant fingers crossed that I had allowed enough time margin for the train to clear the section without any delay to a following train) and some I turned into the goods loop from the main line.

My last train on that shift was the 6.05p.m. fitted vacuum freight up from Fishguard, then I emptied the ashes, filled the coal buckets, and swept up. It was with relief that I saw the cycle lamp of my early turn colleague, Pat Ware, bobbing up and down as he came towards the box. The kettle was boiling on the fire, and it was only a matter of changing over, signing the train register and going home.

The weeks passed without any problems, and I came back on the Sunday afternoon, after a couple of hours in bed, to take over the box which I had left eight hours before, switching in expecting a quiet easy afternoon and evening, with time to polish the floor and levers, and clean the windows. Then, I heard a noise which was quite out of place with the normal sounds of a signal box, a faint plaintive squeak from downstairs. At first I thought it was a dry signal wire riding over a dry pulley, but when the frame had settled down from my reversing signals after switching in, it came again, and I began to be concerned that I might have a signal wire on the point of breaking. When a wire did break, as I was to find out many times in the future, it would not be a slow affair with plenty of warning, it would go with a bang and send me flying across the signal box. I slid back the window and had a look outside, and the squeak came again from under the wooden boards covering the point rodding. I went down the stairs, lay down full length on the path, and looked under those boards, where I found a friend, a tiny grey and white kitten, dirty, wet and almost dead. As I lifted it out it curled up into the palm of my hand like a little sodden ball of dirty wool, chilled through almost to the point of extinction.

I took the kitten up into the box, but had to leave it for a moment laid on the polished lino, as I dealt with a train. I pulled off the signals, booked the train in the register, then went back to the kitten which had not moved or cried out. I sorted through the cleaning cupboard and found some dry rags which I made into a pad, then I placed the kitten on it and laid it in front of the fire. There was no movement for the next hour, then as the warmth crept through that small body, the remaining spark of life began to flicker into a small flame, the kitten opened its eyes, opened its tiny pink mouth and let out a faint cry.

That day I was to go without any milk in my tea, I had brought enough for a couple of brew-ups, but I poured the milk into a saucer and stood it on top of the oven. When it had warmed through, I began an operation that was to last for days and to be shared by my mates on the other turns of duty. Picking the kitten up, I dipped my finger in the milk and began to dribble some into its mouth — a long laborious job, until eventually it was all gone, then I mashed up a little corned beef from my sandwiches and managed to get some nourishment into that little cat.

When it was time to switch out at 10.00p.m. it was with some concern, because my mate coming on in the morning would have no knowledge of our new recruit. I left him a note and placed the kitten in a cardboard box behind the stove, where it promptly went to sleep, not even knowing that I was gone.

When I came back on duty the next afternoon I brought food and bedding for the kitten, but I could hardly believe my eyes when I climbed the stairs into the box, for that kitten was dancing and charging all over the floor chasing its shadow and anything else that moved, and it was clean too, for my mate had gently washed it in some warm water in the hand basin, and he too had given up his milk. I had brought enough to last until the next day, because, of course, the night man would be unaware of the kitten. Looking back on it now, it must have been a laughable sight in Milton signal box, to see three grown men spending every minute between trains crouched down, or sat in a chair, concentrating on getting the kitten to lick their milky fingers. One day, after several weeks of nursemaiding and constant devoted attention, it began to lap up milk and eat, and at last we all knew that we had won.

Susie, as we named her, grew sleek and fat, and she had the best of everything. When Harry Payne, the ganger, hit a key a mile away, she would be up on her hind legs looking down the line with the sure knowledge that he would have some titbit for her, and in the summer she would sit out in the sun on the window-sill, sedately watching the trains go by, aloof from it all, queen of all she surveyed.

She became a familiar figure to the train crews, and when the summer holiday traffic started, excited children would see this cat perched up on the window-sill and they would tug at their parents' arms, pulling them urgently towards the window to see her. In time, she grew wise of the way of train movements, and she would cross the running lines to hunt in the fields opposite only when the signals were back in the frame. She remained with us for three years, then within a short period of time we all moved on and left her, and so she went too; her three 'mums' had gone and there was nothing to keep her, so one night she slipped away and never returned.

I settled in at Milton, and apart from the day-to-day working, various emergencies arose as they did at every signalbox, mostly little things that were dealt with as they cropped up, such as hot boxes, tail lamps out on the last vehicle, and failures in the section. Then one afternoon there was a fault on my block instrument, when the 1.18p.m. out of Paddington was offered to me by Bill Ackrill at Foxhall, and I was unable to give him 'line clear', which meant that Bill could not pull off his advanced starting signal because it was locked by my instrument.

There was nothing I could do except send for the signal linesman. I got the 'line clear' from Steventon and pulled off my signals, but poor old Bill had an awkward time of it, until the block had been repaired, because he had to stop every down train and verbally instruct the driver to pass the advanced starting signal under rule 38 (b). 'Instruct' under these circumstances is something of a misnomer. The drill was to go to the window with a megaphone and bellow one's lungs out against the roar of a 'Castle' or 'King' with a nice big fire in her box blowing her head off from the safety valve, then the fireman had to come to the box, which meant further delay.

The next train down was the 1.55p.m. from Paddington, which ran fast to Reading, then non-stop to Newport; she took six minutes to pass me instead of the usual one, with 5020 *Trematon Castle* blasting her chimney almost off to get some run into thirteen coaches again. However, the signal linesman was quick on the repair job, he cycled down from Didcot and had my instrument repaired by 3.40p.m., so Bill could rest his voice after that.

We notified District Inspector Bill Checkley, and the local controller at Didcot East Junction that no more delays were forthcoming. The controller was relieved because he had a very onerous job, and one that I would not wish to do. The controller on my shift was Bill Churchman, one of nature's gentlemen, who had been a signalman for some time, but with the build-up of traffic it had become necessary to create this controller grade to take some of the load off the signalmen in the district. Bill's job at Didcot East Junction gave him supreme control over all movements, and together with two signalmen and a booking boy, he had the overall picture of all trains on the main lines, relief lines, the Oxford branch avoiding loops, the Newbury branch, the goods yard and locomotive shed, and all the station movements, so a priority of movement could be made.

Bill worked in close contact with all the signalmen in the district as well as the Reading Control. For instance, he would advise me of the routing of Up goods traffic with suggestions as to how it should run. He could have given a direct order, but that wasn't Bill's way, because with the running of Up goods there was sometimes a chance to run one main line on a tight margin in front of an Up express. Bill would have been given the departure time of the goods from Swindon, so allowing for good running he would ring me up for information, and I would check back down the line to my mates in the signal boxes at Wantage and Challow. Sometimes we knew the drivers and their way of running, then I could go back to Bill and inform him that this train was running well and that we could allow it to carry on, and Bill, knowing of my experience of footplate working would take my word and allow a run-through.

Both Foxhall Junction and Didcot East Junction had the passing times of all Up trains wired to them, so we could see how things were brewing up and act accordingly, and of course, it worked the other way. Highworth Junction and Challow would enquire about the running of Down trains and work their margin out the same way. My standard telephone duties were in advising Reading Control of all Up trains, and also special attention was made on Down passenger trains clearing Steventon, because this was leaving the London division, and as long as they cleared Steventon on time, any delays could not be blamed on London, that would be Bristol's job to sort out. My mate at Steventon had the reverse of this, any trains clearing me were out of the Bristol area and became our responsibility, so we were very much in demand from Reading and Bristol Controls.

My first real emergency came after three months at Milton, and it was one which could have had serious consequences but for the skill and correct handling of a goods train by the driver. I had come on duty for the late shift at 2.00p.m. and my first Down passenger, the 1.15p.m. from Paddington, was running on the Down main line while a train of empty coal wagons, from Old Oak Common on their way to Aberdare, was running alongside on the Down loop, both trains approaching my signals together. I stood at the frame ready to place back the signals once the trains had passed, and as I looked back towards them I could see the goods train behaving in a most peculiar manner, wagons jumping about sending up a cloud of coal dust, then the passenger train drew alongside blotting out the goods. When the passenger train was past, I could see what had happened. The goods train had half a dozen wagons off the rails, but the driver had spotted this and kept them going with a tight coupling until the passenger was safely past.

Now the rules and regulations came into action, I placed the signals back, cleared the block back to Foxhall for the Down passenger, then sent him the six bells 'Obstruction Danger' and placed the instrument to 'Train on line', so that no more could come that way. However, a situation was arising on the Up main line while this was going on. An Aberdare coal train was hammering up the main line towards me, and if I slapped the signals back into the face of this lad, he had no chance at all of stopping in time, and although he might have a try, he would most certainly knock the guard flying in his van. My experience as an ex-footplate man helped me in assessing the situation in a case like this: I could see that the Down goods with the derailed wagons was coming to a stand with the wagons upright, so I let the Up train run, judging that there was no likelihood that the derailment would foul the Up running line.

I notified Reading Control, Bill Churchman at Didcot East Junction, and Bill Checkley my District Inspector, and the latter told me to start making arrangements for using the Up main line for single line working. I replied, with all of three months experience, that I thought we could get away without resorting to this and avoid the consequent heavy delays. He went quiet for a minute, and said he would be with me soon, and I wondered if I had put my head on the chopping block with my last statement. Single line working with all its attendant delays, was a long drawn out affair, and I had the 1.55p.m. out of Paddington to come, first stop Newport, then the 2.30p.m. for Gloucester, so I hoped we could avoid single line working. Ten minutes after I had rung him, Bill Checkley arrived on the station pilot engine, which I signalled down to the box and over the cross-over, then sent him back to Didcot; Bill had dropped off at the home signal with a District Relief Signalman, so he had taken some notice of what I had said.

Bill took a long hard look at that derailment, those half dozen wagons sat there squarely with their wheels on the ballast, in no way were they going to tip over, although half a mile of the Down goods loop was chewed up behind them where the wagon wheels had ridden over the sleepers. Bill came to the box and agreed that I could clear the 'Obstruction Danger' from the block instrument and accept trains down the main line again. He telephoned and made arrangements for the breakdown gang to come, and left the Relief Signalman at my Home signal, all trains being slowed down to walking pace past the derailment on the instructions from my mate on the ground.

The goods train which had caused all the trouble was quickly dealt with. The guard uncoupled behind the last wagon that remained on the rails, and the engine and wagons pulled forward, clear of my outgoing loop points. By now I had the breakdown train on the Down main line, then backed it in to the derailed wagons, and with the use of jacks and plates those wagons were back on the rails in no time. Out came the breakdown gang, through the cross-over and up the main line to Didcot, while the goods engine backed on and completed his train again. Once coupled up, he was allowed to proceed slowly to Steventon and detach the defective wagons for examination. It was all over by 5.30p.m. leaving me the highly polished floor now looking like a ploughed field, but, I had been blooded, now I really was a signalman, and Bill Checkley had seen me operate under pressure and was satisfied.

All it needed was for me to get a uniform! Events had moved so fast between leaving the footplate and joining the box that the uniform just hadn't caught up with me, although I had been measured three weeks ago, but before the late turn came round in three weeks' time I would be kitted out, because an important event was to take place.

On the Monday of that week, I collected my uniform from Bill Checkley's office, and somehow managed to carry it on the handlebar of my bike back to Milton. It was a lovely issue, pure Great Western with brass buttons everywhere, and included two pairs of trousers, two long-sleeved waistcoats, two jackets, one heavy overcoat, and one stiff peaked cap. This cap was the only item that seemed superfluous: it was placed in the bottom of my locker and remained there gathering dust, indeed, I can't remember any signalman wearing one. Relief men had to wear one when carrying out the duties of Pilotman for single line working, or during the relaying of track or renewing signals, when they were acting as ground signalmen. The remainder of the uniform was good stuff, a far cry from my old footplate overalls and cap, and most of us took a pride in it, brushing and pressing, and polishing the GWR buttons until we would have done credit to a Guardsman. I still have a tin full of buttons, a little tarnished now, but genuine Great Western brass, and something to hang onto as a reminder of those golden days.

I took the trousers, jacket and waistcoat home with me that evening, so that on Tuesday when I arrived on duty I would look every inch a signalman. When a 'Royal' was booked through, I belonged, not that I would be noticed any more than Harry Payne, the ganger, who kept me company, or the relaying gang stretched out along the section, spaced out half a mile apart until the 'Royal' had passed. But there was another reason for getting me kitted out on this late turn. It was discovered that Milton box had never been passed out by the Ministry of Transport, so the official passing-out was to be performed on the Thursday, and I just happened to be the signalman on duty. My mates on the other turns were pleased to be clear of all this expected 'top brass', and I was not too happy about it either, not being exactly scared, just having the wind up a bit. On that afternoon when I relieved the early turn man, he was out of the box and gone in a flash although the Inspection train wasn't due until after the 1.15 p.m. from Paddington had gone through. As this passed, I cleared the section and accepted the Inspection train, stopping it dead at my home signal before changing the points over for the loop line and allowing it to clear the main line.

The little 14XX class tank engine with its one coach came to a stand opposite the box, and I could see down into that Inspection coach, where there were tables laid out with white linen, silver cutlery, glasses and bottles and a white-coated attendant. These Inspection blokes certainly were doing themselves all right, I thought to myself. They all piled out with not a backward glance at the bulled-up little locomotive (perhaps they imagined it always looked like that?) and came towards the signal box. I began to tick off the people that I knew. There were some familiar faces, Bill Checkley, Freddie Blackhall and Chief Inspector Honeybone, all resplendent in their number one uniform, gold braid and gleaming brass buttons in every direction. Then came Mr. Grand, the General Manager, looking very smart in a well-cut suit and bowler hat, and trailing along behind came a civilian gentleman wearing a trilby hat, whom I had never seen before.

I had a last quick look around the signal-box, the windows were clean, the floor highly polished, the levers gleamed like chrome plating, the brass release plungers shone, the stove had been black-leaded, even the coal buckets too, so there was nothing left to bring discredit to Milton box.

Bill Checkley introduced me, Freddie Blackhall winked, Mr. Honeybone whispered that everything was all right, and then I met the General Manager whom up until now, I had only seen in photographs in the Great Western magazine, naming locomotives. Then he introduced me to the man in the trilby hat, Lt. Col. Wilson from the Inspectorates Office of the Ministry of Transport. To say that I was surprised would be an understatement, for this civilian that I shook hands with was not my idea of a full-blown high-ranking army officer. I had met enough of these gentlemen when firing the many troop trains, and they had all been big men, usually with red tabs on their tunic collars, and with a host of lesser officers hovering in the background, but this man was slightly built with a little sandy moustache under his nose. He stood watching me deal with the trains on the block, gently asking questions as to my railway background, and was most interested to learn about my footplate experiences. Once the block had been cleared, he asked my permission to take over, and I stood back to see him pick up the lever cloth and go through that frame so fast, testing locking, signals, points and instruments that even I would have been hard pressed to keep up with him, so I was obviously in the presence of an expert.

Satisfied with the result, he gave me back my signal box, and the others began to prepare to leave, but this great man would have none of it. He pressed me more about footplate work, then he wanted to know about my transfer, and my rapid progress through the Reading School into this job, turning to Chief Inspector Honeybone for confirmation, and he made the point of remarking that it would be a good thing if there was an interchange of jobs on the operating side.

There was a general discussion up in the corner, and hand-shaking all round, then they went clattering down the stairs and back to the little train, leaving Bill Checkley behind. I turned the train out on to the main line, right away to Swindon.

Bill sat down and had a cup of tea with me, he was glad that this inspection was over, and that it had gone off correctly, and now he began to open up and reveal that behind those frosty features was a real nice bloke. He talked about his time in the Household Cavalry, and the spit and polish that went behind the ceremonial troopings, and of his railway years in a signal box, and of course his pet subject, growing roses. It was a good job that he mentioned that, because a few weeks later his hobby almost became his undoing; I was cycling up the path on the way home when I heard a cry for help across on the Down loop side, and laid down my bike and crossed the running lines to find Bill trapped face down in a bramble bush. He had gone in after a briar that he had been training for months to grow in a straight line, and he had dug it out by the roots when he became tangled up, unable to move. I pulled him out by his feet, leaving bits of his skin here and there, but he emerged triumphant, clutching that briar with such a pleased look about him.

At Milton, stuck out in the middle of the countryside, it was surprising to see that there was always something going on if one used one's eyes. Through the rear window I could look out over Didcot Depot, which has now been swept away to make way for the giant power station. It was worth a look through that window now and again, over the vast expanse of railway network stretching for miles between the various storage sheds, with pannier tanks bustling about, and I knew every inch of those tracks from my firing days, and it was to come in handy at a later date to overcome a very big problem.

The activities of one of the staff kept me interested for weeks. Behind the shed opposite the signal box was a large stack of wooden wheel barrows, and each morning this chap would come out with a little compressor and a paint spray gun, and spray the barrows army grey, working his way quietly through the pile. During the dinner break, he would change the colour of the paint in the spray gun to black and get to work spraying a new grey army bike which would dry off during the afternoon. At five in the evening he would mount it and ride off.

One of the War Department police officers came round the fence one day, and exchanging the state of the weather with him, he happened to mention that army bikes were being pinched; I kept well out of the matter, just wishing I could have had one of those bikes myself. They did catch him of course, months later, with a pound of nails in his dinner bag, and they took the nails off him and then watched him ride away on a black bike!

The best friends that a signalman could have, apart from his mates in the other boxes, were the permanent way ganger and his men, and in this respect I was lucky, as my district ganger, Harry Payne, and all the platelayers were the best bunch of men you could wish to meet. I would see Harry every day except on the night shift, he would come out of his cottage at Steventon

41

each morning, rain or shine, a bag full of wooden keys and liners on his back, and his big key hammer over his shoulder. He would walk his length, up the Down main against the traffic, looking for cracked or broken rails, driving keys back into the rail chairs if they were out, and replacing those that were missing. In the afternoon he would walk back on the Up main line doing the same, joining the platelayers wherever they were working in the section. He had immense pride in his job, and as a result, had a prize section, the examination train never dropped a dollop of whitewash anywhere on *his* sleepers. On a hot summer morning I could tell that Harry was on the way just by listening, for long before he came into sight under the bridge, I would hear the 'wang' of the rails as he drove in a key, and by the time he reached me, it was time for a sit down and a cup of tea, but not for long, because Harry would soon be itching to move on, never wasting a minute of the company's time.

It used to be a source of wonder to me to see some of these old gangers at work. Although they had no formal engineering training, they could measure up a complicated junction that was due for renewal, send off the measurements, and a couple of months later an engineering occupation on a Sunday would see the old track lifted out by a steam crane, and the new section go in without a change even of half an inch.

Sometimes Harry would come up into the box and inform me that he had found a broken rail in the section, and it was a case of us both working closely together so as not to cause any undue delay to trains. I would give Harry a time between trains (usually he would require about half an hour) then, until that time came round, Harry would round up his gang, place a new rail on the platelayer's trolley, and they would all go post-haste to the breakage, pushing the trolley loaded with rail, shovels and picks, where they would then commence to slack off the fish-plate bolts where necessary.

If Harry was close to one of the loop line telephones, he would ring me to see if it was all right to start the job, but, if he was way out in the section, we used our pre-arranged system of communication. I would lower and raise the nearest signal to him, and Harry would go into action and the gang, spread out along the affected rail, would swing their key hammers knocking out the keys, lift out the rail, and replace it with the new one, and as soon as it was resting inside the chairs, the keys would be hammered back in, and the fish-plate bolts tightened up. I always gave Harry

42

a good margin to complete this operation, and always with a proviso that should he be running tight on time, I would raise and lower the signal five minutes before I needed the section handed back, but in fact, I never once had to use that five minute reminder.

The platelayers in the gang of course spent all their time out in the various parts of the section, and months might pass before I saw them, while at other times, the area of maintenance would be within the signals, and I would have their company for some time. Three of them had duties connected with my signal box, and these chaps were my fogmen, but the whole gang turned out in the snow, to keep the points and signal free of ice. Fog working was one of the worst aspects of signal box work, throwing an immense strain on the signalman. With all visibility gone, particularly at night, we would 'fly on the instruments' as an airline pilot would say, watching the diagram, track circuits and signal repeaters, and, as a double safety measure, we would introduce double block working — that is to say, we would not give 'line clear' to the box in the rear, until we had received 'line clear' from the box in advance. We had our terms of reference before introducing this system of working, namely, if we could not see our home signals, but we also consulted together by a telephone call to our mates all up and down the line, and then we would all send for the fogmen. If the fog came down during normal daylight working hours, they would report to the box anyway, but at night or during the early hours, a porter would be dispatched from the nearest station to knock them up.

My three chaps would report to me, then I would enter their names and the time of reporting in the train register book, and off two of them would go. Harry Woodbridge went to my Down distant signal and Bill Strong to my Up distant, and providing that the distant signal was in the off position for oncoming trains, they would take no action. If the Distant signal was at the caution position, they would place one fog detonator on the rail to be exploded by the wheels of the train, and also at the same time exhibit a yellow light to the driver, from a hand-held oil lamp.

This was a god-forsaken job on a dirty night, stuck miles out in the section in the fog, working from a little wooden hut for shelter. Admittedly, they had a little stove inside, but for months at a time these huts were out of use, and so became damp and most uncomfortable. I always made a point of having some dry wood and a lump of paraffin-soaked cotton waste ready for my fogmen to take, plus a small sack of dry coal, which was only a little thing to do, but much appreciated by my lads.

The third chap had the most enviable of jobs. His duty was to stay in the box with me and look for tail lamps, because in the fog it was a very difficult job to see a tail lamp on the last vehicle, and without seeing it, we could not clear the section behind and accept another train. If, by chance, the tail lamp was out, then it meant waiting until the train had been stopped and an examination made to make sure that the last vehicle on the train was indeed there, then the message passed back to the last signal box before 'train out of section' could be given.

Goods trains were no problem. By the time 70 odd wagons had passed by, the smoke and steam had cleared and the three lamps carried on the brake van could easily be seen, but with passenger trains it was very difficult. Many drivers were loath to run hard, so with the regulator eased down, the smoke and steam from the chimney would roll back along the coaches, mingle with the leaks from the steam heating pipes on the coaches, and tuck up behind the last vehicle, which was already becoming invisible as the fog swirled in behind. My chap out of the gang for this duty was 'Pecker' Strong, and I could not have had a better bloke to help me. He was quite within his rights to remain in the box and lean out of the window looking for tail lamps, as we both did in any case to confirm our sightings, but, if the fog was very thick, 'Pecker' would be down on the ground making sure, shouting up his confirmation to me so that I could clear the section with the least delay. None of these lads complained about the job, although sometimes after a hard day's work out in the section, they would get home and only have time to snatch a meal, before they had to be back again for a full night's duty. They were all professional railwaymen, devoted to keeping the trains running, and to this end, they used to put up with the most atrocious conditions.

Fog was certainly an inconvenience, but it was the snow that caused the real problems. When the airlines shut down, and the buses stopped running, there was still one way of moving people and goods, and that was the railway. I can never remember the railways coming to a complete halt, but it was only because of the platelayers working until they dropped, to keep the points and signals free from ice. It was heart-breaking to see them hunched up over a pair of points, scraping and brushing snow out of the slides with a blizzard blowing up their tail, then standing back to let an express pass, and finding afterwards, that the rush of air from the train had blown the snow back in again. I used to help from the box as much as I could by keeping the points and signals on the move to prevent them from freezing, and I insisted that one at a time they came to the box to thaw out, and have a hot drink, every half an hour or so, and in return for those small considerations, hardly a week went by without my receiving a gift of a rabbit or a cabbage, and in the spring, young onions for the salad.

During normal weather conditions, the gangers had a short shift on a Saturday morning, oiling the points and locking bars, and we in the signal box, would help in this operation, by moving the parts to be oiled as they requested. One side of the point slides would be oiled, then they would wave their arm slowly backwards and forwards in front, as a sign to change the points over so that the opposite slide could be dealt with. For the locking bars, the arm was raised up and down; the system worked beautifully, and it was always a delight to find how easily those points worked after the Saturday treatment.

One little game we used to play on them, was when they came to oil near to the box. It had to be near so that we were on top of them and could see what they were doing. The oil feeder for this job was a big one with a very long spout, so we would watch the spout go into the open points, then a quick snatch on the lever would squeeze the end of the oil feeder flat before they could get it out, and they were obliged to go over to the platelayers' hut and get out a hacksaw, to take off half an inch from the spout, before they could start again. Every platelayers' hut carried a large stock of short-spouted oil feeders, but they took it all in good spirits, providing that this bit of fun was not carried out too often.

At the start of each period for which a new timetable was issued, one of us would pick out the trains relevant to that particular box during the full twenty four hours, and stick a list of them on the wall over the register, but constant use over the first few weeks made this list superfluous until the next change of timetables. My first experience of this came with the change from the winter service to the summer service, which always began on the first of May, and I was introduced to it by the time-honoured method of delivery to out station signal boxes on the Great Western. I was on the 6.00a.m. early shift when the first Down stopping passenger train came towards me blowing the whistle, so I slid open the window to see the guard fling out a bundle that went bouncing along the Up main line. When I had collected this bundle and opened it up, it proved to be the new service timetables for the summer months. It took me several hours to re-write our list, checking with the other lads down the line to see if we had missed any trains out, and when it was completed, I could see that this was going to be a busy time. There were many extra trains, particularly on a Saturday, holiday trains from Newcastle to Bournemouth, Poole, Weymouth and Weston-super-Mare, and, of course, the returns, and the normal Up traffic was booked to run in two or three parts. When the summer service started, the West Curve at Foxhall was a very busy place, and many goods trains were either blocked back until the night hours, or cancelled, for with all the extra trains mixed up with the ordinary booked service, there was just no margin for goods traffic. I doubt if there were many locomotives or crews available either, all the 'Halls' and 'Granges' being in use, and even the old Churchward 'forty-threes' sported 'A' headlamps for a change.

To an outsider it would have seemed an impossible situation to sort out at junctions, and 'boxers' were flying about all over the place. 'Boxers' was the name for box-to-box messages, and an example would be 'the first part of the Fishguard preceding the second part of the Weston'. When such a telephone message was received from Steventon, I would pass it on to Foxhall Junction, and so it would go on, all the way up the line to Paddington, and it would apply to the Down line as well, so a tight watch on the timetable had to be kept to sort out the confusion. It was up to the junction signalman to sort everything out, and at times it proved impossible, so trains got mixed up by running out of sequence. If there was any doubt, the signals would be pulled off for the main line and if the driver stopped we would change the points over and try him that way, working on the theory that the driver, at least, should know what train he was driving, and which way he wanted to go! One of these 'boxers' was a regular one, even in the winter, and this was the one about the 8.00 a.m. up from Cheltenham, because it regularly carried the Chairman, General Sir Brian Robertson. He would get in the train quite unaware that the signalman was looking out for him, then the message would go ahead from box to box, and we all made sure that this express had a clear run. When Sir Brian got to Paddington he made a point of thanking the driver for a good run, little knowing how it was achieved, but the drivers did however, and always gave a 'thumbs up' sign to thank us.

The telephone system was one of the most simple systems devised. In the big boxes there were banks of them, but I only had six in Milton box, four on the wall and one on each side of the block instrument shelf which were direct lines to the boxes on either side of me. The through 'phones worked on a code with a centre selector set in the cabinet, all of the boxes were listed with their code, so if I wanted to ring down the line, I would turn the selector to the appropriate number on the dial and press the selector the correct number of times. An advantage was that this system was an open line so that every signalman right down to Swindon could be on the line at the same time, and that way we were able to keep tabs on the running of every train. It could be a bit of a giggle at times, for instance we might all be linked up having a chat in between trains, and then perhaps a goods train could be heard rattling through Shrivenham with a hot axle box squealing away, so Shrivenham would tell Uffington, he would have a look and decide that it was not too bad and inform Challow, who would pass it on to Wantage, nobody wanting to stop this train with all the attendant work of detaching a wagon and writing out a report. By the time it reached Steventon my mate there would decide that as it had come so far another few miles wouldn't hurt, so Didcot would have the job.

There was no safety risk involved, as we were all aware of the running powers of a hot grease box, and the driver would be keeping an eye on it, as he didn't want to stop with a heavy goods train, but when a grease box became a 'flamer' then action was taken at once. A 'flamer' was quite a show at night, flames whipping out from the axle box with red drops of molten grease splashing out all over the sleepers, and when this happened, the bell code for 'Stop and examine train' would be sent to the box ahead, and this signalman would stop any train going into the section until the defective train had come to a standstill.

Every morning we would all be on the telephone from five minutes to eleven waiting for the time signal, and the young lady in the exchange would be linked up with both us and Paddington. It was most important that we did not miss this appointment, because the moment the clock at Paddington reached eleven o'clock, the young lady would call out over the telephone, 'it's eleven o'clock' so that every signal box was operating on Paddington time. This signal had to be entered in the register with any alteration made to the signal box clock, and so much impor- tance was placed on the ritual, that each month when the District Inspector made his routine visit, he would check back through the book to see that the clock had been booked every day. All guards on passenger trains were expected to correct their watches with the Paddington clock so that those country stations that were without a signal box could obtain the correct time from the guard on the first train out of Paddington that stopped at the station. In that way, the whole of the Great Western ran on Paddington time, and so, the accuracy of times when trains passed in and out of the various divisions were confirmed, and in the unfortunate event of an accident, the actual time of occurrence could be recorded. Such was the importance to me of this standard time, that even today, thirty years later, I cannot tolerate a clock being wrong, the time has to be the correct time. In fact, when we were newly married, it used to drive my dear wife 'up the wall' if our clocks were slow or fast at home, because I would fiddle for days with the regulator until I was satisfied that the time was correct. Dear girl, she has got used to it now, and accepts it as one of my little ways that I can't get out of.

As that first summer at Milton wore on, I began to settle down and enjoy life, and I found that I did not have to stop and think or work out margins for freight trains; the job became easier, and I was dealing with it in an unhurried way, fully confident. I had seen my share of ordinary emergencies, and I had dealt with a derailment, so now I began to plan for the long term. I had the rule book out and the appendix, laid on the desk so that I could go through it at every opportunity. In any case, we all had to keep on top of the operating rules so as to pass the yearly examination by the District Inspector, but I had plans for the future, and any small alteration that came along, I carefully stuck inside my book so that it was always up to date. On the telephone, I would discuss rules with any of the other lads who were interested, wanting to be sure that I could answer any question that was thrown at me, but there had to be an incentive for all that knowledge I was cramming in, and there was, because I was getting married, and I wanted promotion to a higher class signal box, with the extra money, just as soon as I could.

The wedding was all fixed up for August, and as the time drew near I had so much advice about married life from the lads all down the line, that I could not possibly fail to be a good husband. My young lady went home to Wales a month before to prepare for the wedding, and I had a lieu day owing to me for working on a bank holiday, so that would give me the Friday off in addition to a week's holiday for our honeymoon. On the Friday afternoon I caught the train from Didcot, heading for Swindon and Newport (changing trains at both places), then on to Abertillery and the church. I stood in the corridor as far as Swindon, as I had promised the lads that I would, and they were waiting for me, standing at the windows of their boxes all the way from Didcot West End. Some were swinging small axes, to signify that I was going to get the chop, some were wiping dry tears from their eyes, and some were pointing their thumbs down, the Roman sign to the gladiator, to show that I was doomed.

Changing trains at Swindon brought back many memories of steam days. As I waited for the South Wales express to arrive, a dirty old 72XX class tank came knocking her way through the middle road, with a long rake of wagons, her fireman pulling the fire through with the pricker, sweat was pouring off him as he struggled in the enclosed cab on that hot afternoon. I felt sorry for him, reflecting that, but for my transfer, that could have been me. As soon as the brake van was clear the South Wales express ran in, a scruffy 'Castle' at the head of thirteen coaches. The blower was on, and this fireman too was sweating hard as he leaned out of the cab, his face black with coal dust, a weary look about him. I climbed into the coach behind the tender, and as I sat down I could hear the scrape of the shovel as it rode on the tender plate. Poor blighter, he was firing in the station, and with the blower on it implied a rough trip. I sat back with a feeling of smugness, secure in the knowledge that I had left all that behind, and yet I was wondering in the back of my mind if I should go and offer him a hand. However, before I could talk myself into it, the whistle blew and we were off. Rough engine or not, we made good time to Newport, and when I got out of the coach the fireman was pulling the pricker through the fire, ready for going to shed at Cardiff. With my case in my hand, I crossed the footbridge to the opposite platform, then made my way back towards the end of the platform where the valley trains stood.

There were always two trains waiting, one for the Eastern valley and one for the Western valley, and not always in the right order, so it was as well to check with the driver. I had learnt that the hard way a few weeks before, when with the superiority of a railwayman who thought he had no need to ask questions, I got in the wrong train and landed up at Ystrad Mynach. It had taken two bus rides and a taxi to find my way to Abertillery, quite a feat for an Englishman stranded in the depths of rural Wales. So this time, I walked up the length of the rear train that was buffered up to the train in front, and spoke to the driver, whose reply was 'noo, mun, I'm Eastern, the boyo in front is for the Western valley'. I thanked him and walked on towards the head of the train, looking for a compartment on my own. There were four coaches this time, quite a load for the little 57XX class pannier tank, and finding a compartment next to the engine I climbed in and was about to place my case in the rack when a voice came in through the open window. 'Arrald, bach, what are you dooing year?' I turned round and found myself looking at Jim Bevin, one of my old mates from my footplate days. During the time since I had become a signalman, Jim had returned to Wales, so it was a pleasure to meet an old comrade out of the blue like that. Jim pulled my leg unmercifully about going up the valley to be married, then he dared me to ride on the footplate with him to Abertillery, and I thought why not, because I could ride in a coach any time, but I hadn't been on the footplate for months, not since firing that farm special back in February.

Now it occurred to me that a 57XX class pannier tank is not the roomiest place to be on a hot August evening, and I now came out with a suggestion that was stupid, but it was done on the spur of the moment, never dreaming that it would be taken up. Why ride on the footplate as a passenger, why not fire the engine and let the fireman ride in the coach? Jim agreed, it would give me a chance to see what valley work was all about, so off came my jacket to join the case on the rack, and I jumped down onto the platform again. The fireman didn't need to be offered this opportunity twice, he pressed a ball of cotton waste in my hand and was in the compartment in a flash.

I rolled up my sleeves and tucked my tie in my pocket, then tucked my trousers into the top of my socks. There was just time to have a look at the enormous fire in the fire box, it must have been a couple of feet thick, then doors began slamming and whistles blowing. Jim blew off the brakes, placed the lever in fore gear, and at 6.50p.m. we were off, clattering over points and crossovers, and under the road bridge. I had just lifted the bunker flap when we plunged into the darkness of Newport tunnel, the light from the fire showing the coal pouring down to cover my shoes, and filling my socks with small coal, which I could feel between my toes, just like being at the seaside with a shoe full of sand. We came bouncing out of that tunnel into the sunshine, so I began to fire her, then there was an almighty lurch as we turned right and headed up a bank towards Bassaleg, causing me to stagger and scattering the coal from my shovel all over the footplate. I got up from my sitting position on the floor boards, and scraped the coal up, then it was time to put on the injector, and leave it on, for that little engine was using up water faster than I was used to. Jim linked the valve gear up a couple of notches and gave her a bit more with the regulator, and I began to fire again, wondering whether I was ever going to see what was going on, as the firing seemed to be non-stop. Then Jim shut the regulator and we ran into Bassaleg, seven minutes out of Newport.

One minute of station time and we were off again, and I began firing, down with the flap, in with the coal, up with the flap, over and over again, that little tank engine scoffing up the coal as fast as I could put it in, without even the chance to shout a few words to Jim over the chattering of the exhaust. Then he shut off again and we were running into Rogerstone, sweeping past the great yards full of loaded coal wagons, and Rogerstone loco shed, packed with big 72XX, 42XX, tanks, and dozens of Churchward 'twenty-eights'. We stopped for one minute at Rogerstone and then we were off again, climbing now up into the mountains, the sun casting shadows, covering the sides of the valley with a soft green and brown hue as the fern growth changed colour towards the coming autumn. Now that the boiler was at a respectable level, and the fire burning well, I could spare the time to look outside the cab, to hear the chimney chattering away, and to see our silhouette reflected back. It was all so new to me; the view from the coach was appreciated and then forgotten, but from the footplate, that little pannier tank engine began to show me another aspect of the valley, something I could not appreciate when riding in a coach, the nature of the line ahead, twisting, turning, climbing, passing whistle boards every hundred yards, now having to slow down for a subsidence, now to open up again, the engine responding like a fussy little terrier, but still climbing ever up and through the valleys between the mountains. I could look down at the rows of miners' cottages, rows and rows of terraces, each home a couple of feet above the next one, all with slate roofs and dingy stone walls, each with a line of snow-white washing fluttering in the soft breeze, and I could see the dark River Ebbw tumbling over rocks and boulders as it hastened down the valley towards the sea.

I returned to my firing, the injector still on and forgotten, that little engine needing every bit of coal and water that I could put into her. We tore on with the urgency of the tightest timing that I had ever come across, scoffing coal and water at an alarming rate, equal to that of a 'Hall' on the main line with ten coaches on. We stopped at all stations, Tynycwn Halt, Risca, Cross Keys, Cwncarn, Abercarn, Newbridge, wasting no time at any, and we ran into Crumlin Low Level only thirty-three minutes after leaving Newport, to stand at the end of the platform under the spindly legs of the viaduct striding over the valley above us. I just had time to bend down into the corner of the cab and shut off the injector water feed and we were off again, the urgent blast of the whistle confirming the guard's 'right away'. Five minutes to Llanhileth, sweeping past the signal box in the lee of the mountain which towered above it, while the loco shed was tucked up in the corner between the main line and the mountain on the other side of the valley. Round the corner ahead, I could see the outskirts of Abertillery, and yet there were two more stops before I could leave this fussy, brave little engine. It was a three minute ride to Aberbeeg, and a booked stop for water, and here the line to Ebbw Vale curved away to the left of us, to disappear in the shadow of the mountain. The fireman came out of the coach and clambered up onto the tank, the lid clip was knocked back and the leather water bag dropped in, then water began to gush into her tanks, all done with the slick practice of familiarity. Five minutes later we were away again; I had finished with the shovel now, and could stand in the cab doorway to allow the cool air to dry the sweat which was streaming down my face. Two minutes brought us to Six Bells Halt, rows of sidings covered with coal dust and stretching back to connect with the colliery, where the tall winding gear overlooked the whole area, and the spinning winding gear wheels were accompanied by the soft 'puff, puff' of escaping steam from the engine house. The rows of terraced houses in serried ranks curved round the side of the mountain and looked down into the town below, down even into the top of the blackened chimney of the foundry, and overlooked the bridge crossing the dirty river, still tumbling its way down the valley. Jim closed the regulator and began to apply the brake. There was just time for me to shake his hand and jump down onto Abertillery platform, grabbing my suitcase and jacket out of the compartment, before he was away again, hammering his way up towards Brynmawr, the echoes of that chattering chimney coming back to me as he rounded the curve and disappeared out of sight. I saw him go, and felt satisfied that I had fired an engine up the valley and now I had some idea of what valley work was all about; it was a rough life, and one that I was thankful was not mine.

The other passengers were making their way over the footbridge and I picked up my case and made my way towards the bridge, to see a shapely pair of legs come down the steps, which could only belong to my Bet, my beautiful young bride of tomorrow who had come to meet me. I put down my case and opened my arms to sweep her off her feet, confident in the knowledge that she loved me, but when she saw me, her features were a mixture of emotions. She had been laying a plan of which I was quite unaware, of walking up through the middle of the town to show off this Englishman that she was about to marry on the morrow. It was to be a slow walk, so that all her friends could see the smart young man that she had spoken so much about, but when she set eyes on me, she had to change her plans. I was black with coal dust, my shoes covered in it, the trousers of my number two suit were crumpled and wet at the knees, and my tie was dangling out of one pocket, my white shirt was filthy, with two large damp sweat stains under my arms, and I had lost two shirt-buttons somewhere, so that the sweat and dust had congealed into a mess of slurry on my chest, and under the coal dust, my face was brick red from the heat of the fire box. She ignored my outstretched arms and backed away; this was no young knight in shining armour riding a white horse, neither was he a clean young off-duty signalman, but looked like a collier just up from the local mines, and it was as well if she stood up-wind of him. We walked in stony silence through the town via the back streets, up through back alley-ways and out into connecting roads. As we passed the 'Lamb' public house, the open door looked most inviting, and a sign on the wall advertised Webb's Golden Ale, cool and fresh from the barrel, and I could have drunk a gallon of it, but now was not the moment. We then began the one in three climb up to Darran Road and her home, conversation being impossible on this steep road in any case.

It took her mother only an hour to get over the shock, long enough for me to climb into a tin bath in the back kitchen with a bar of soap and a scrubbing brush, and while I was in the bath I could hear, through the closed door, some comments being made about marrying a local collier. Time is a great healer, and when I emerged from the kitchen, the repairs had been made, and I was pink, clean, acceptable, and I did not smell any more. She married me the next morning at twelve in the Congregational Church to the ringing of bells, and the sound of the packed ranks of the Male Voice Choir, mixed up with much weeping from the ladies. The congregation included my father, mother, sister and my best man, Roy Saunders, all looking so solemn as the sound of the choir swept over them. Father caught my eye and winked. He had apparently laughed until the tears ran down his face when he had been told of my condition on arrival the day before, and it was only when mother heard the story, that she let out that on *her* wedding day my 'old chap' had been down in the pig-sty with her father, which was where he had hidden the beer, because her mother was dead against drink, although it was said that she wasn't against a drop of her 'one hundred per cent' parsnip wine.

That afternoon, my new wife and I went to catch a train to Weymouth for our honeymoon, and when the little pannier tank swept in and stopped, Bet clung to my arm and pushed me into the compartment before I had a chance even to take note of the engine number, let alone have a word with the driver. At Newport I was hustled over the bridge and with much more haste, pushed into the train for Bristol, almost as if I was going somewhere under escort, and I found myself packed in with a dozen other people, with no chance at all of escaping on to the footplate. At Bristol we had a wait of half an hour, during which I had to sit quiet and behave. We boarded the local train to Westbury, and Bet began to relax, knowing that I was now in a district where no dirty old drivers or firemen knew me, and when we got to Westbury and our last change, we were almost down into the West Country.

Our train came in and I ran back to see the guard, showing him my free railway pass and explaining that I was with my bride, whereupon he unlocked a first-class empty compartment in the coach next to the engine for our benefit. As a good husband should, I stood back to allow Bet to enter first, and just at that moment, from the footplate, came a shout of 'Hey, Harold'. I had no chance to reply, as Bet was out of that compartment and down on the platform in a flash, then she pushed me up inside and the guard locked the door before I fully realised that someone knew me. She was determined not to let me anywhere near the engine on this trip: one would think that my first love was a steam locomotive, and, admittedly, it had been at one time, but now I had another love to keep me warm, and I was a signalman with a nice clean job, I did not smell coming home from work, and it was going to stay that way.

That evening, however, it was my turn to take a firm line, with all the experience of a husband of six hours, as we were walking along the front at Weymouth. Bet looked gorgeous in her going-away clothes, a bloom on her cheeks and a sparkle in her eyes, which was enough to make other young men look at her longingly. They would notice me looking 'daggers' at them and would hastily imply that it was something beyond my wife that they were really interested in. I should have known better than to leave her for a few minutes, but, being trained on the footplate, I was used to six cups of tea, which resulted in me disappearing for a while. Five minutes I was away; just five little minutes, and when I came up from underground, my lovely girl had moved away. However, there was a smashing girl leaning up against the sea front railings, but she was obscured from me by a group of American service lads, who were chatting her up. Eventually, one of them moved to one side and I could see that it was MY WIFE who was being chatted up! I said two words, spoken very softly in the ear of one American, such as the Mafia would have said, to get the response that I wanted. He understood English all right, and vanished into the walking crowds with his friends, as quickly as he had appeared. My wife was relieved at their departure, convinced that the husband-to-be of yesterday, was worth a bit more than those four well-heeled Americans.

During that week, we were in the same situation as hundreds of other young couples walking along the sea front. We explored, and sat in the sun, and for five per cent of the time talked about the future, while the other ninety-five per cent introduced me to the harsh realities of married life. This brand new husband was quickly transformed, in that short week, into an old married man. It was done so subtly with all the inborn perceptiveness of a young girl transformed into a married lady, already equipped with plans for a successful marriage. We had been fortunate enough to rent a house to return to; a broken-down old place, it is true, but nevertheless, something that we could turn into a home. I knew that when we got back, there was going to be a spending spree, and we had the pick of all the furniture shops of Reading, Oxford, Swindon, Wallingford and Abingdon, plus a couple of local shops in Didcot, but with the stealth of a huntress, my nice new missus steered me into every furniture shop in Weymouth, not to buy, but as a rehearsal for that operation. This was the reconnaissance patrol to compare prices and to start my education, and in the process I was shown three piece suites, wardrobes, sideboards, dressing tables and chairs of every shape, size and colour. When these shops were exhausted, it was the turn of the fabric shops, to look at bed linen, tea cloths, towels, carpets and curtains, then on to china shops to examine dinner sets, tea sets, knives, forks and saucepans. I was shattered, and thought 'Ye Gods, what could the real thing be like'. On our return home I soon found out, for our hard earned savings went like snow in hot sunshine, together with the motor bike.

I can now look back on that period, knowing that it was a definite turning point in my life: all the rough trips on badly steaming locomotives, and the hectic time I had been through in the last few months, had all failed to do what one very sweet young lady had managed to do in a couple of hours. She had turned the boy into a man, and like all happy couples, we are still cementing the relationship. The colour of curtains, wallpaper, and any replacement to the household equipment is still a topic for debate, but now I can converse on equal terms, having become a very mature wise old married man, highly skilled in the art of agreeing, with the experience of over thirty years behind me to prove that I am right. Doctor Samuel Johnson summed the situation up very nicely, when he said, 'Marriage has many pains, but celibacy has no pleasures'.

We came home after that week, and I returned to Milton on the night shift. I also returned to the comments and well-meant advice from my mates in the other signal boxes. As soon as there was a lull in the traffic, the 'phones began to ring, and the congratulations were given. Advice on how married life should be dealt with swamped me, and everyone was an expert, all being eager to pass on their tips on how to make it a success, how to deal with tap washers, fuses, gardening, laying lino and carpets, and how to stand firm, when to back off, and, of course, the inevitable advice on how to change a baby's napkin. The last piece of advice could only come from one person, Jack Drew in Foxhall Junction box, who had moved round from Didcot North Junction while I had been away, so we now had the 'king' of leg-pullers on our shift, or so he thought at the time.

Jack's reference to nappies was just a start, he had other plans as well. He knew my address, and he passed it round the district. The postman began to call, filling up the hallway with catalogues from every manufacturer of prams, cots and baby clothes in the country; I found out that every signalman had filled in coupons or answered advertisements from every publication that they could lay their hands on!

When this flood of paper work eased off, it was time for me to have my turn, remembering the old saying 'vengeance is sweet'. I gave up spending my spare moments on study of the rule book for a little while, and began to spend a few hours planning revenge, sweet hours they were too, because this had to be something very special. I knew that Jack was partial to a bit of rough shooting, and he had every chance at Foxhall Junction because the box backed on to a small bank with a thicket on the top, a bit of waste ground dividing the West Curve and the Hump shunt spur in Didcot depot. I knew that when Jack was on the night shift, he would tie a torch underneath the barrel of a .22 rifle, and in the early hours when the rabbits came out to feed, he would poke that rifle through the open rear window, switch on the torch and aim between the rabbit's eyes. It was a successful method and he rarely missed, and I was determined not to miss a good opportunity either.

Before one period of night duty, I spent a few minutes of the afternoon in my shed with a milk bottle and a hammer, breaking that bottle into pieces which I collected up and then I set off to work half an hour early. When I got to Foxhall, I propped my bike against the box and swore the late turn signalman to secrecy. I then put that half an hour to good use, as I covered the bank with my little bits of glass, all carefully spaced two inches apart.

My revenge came soon after midnight; I had the Foxhall end of Milton box window open, and in the soft stillness of the night, I could just hear the 'pop, pop' of a rifle, as Jack banged away for hours, because everywhere his torch shone, he could see eyes. At one point he came on the 'phone and said that he had never known so many rabbits about at one time, and he even talked about a contract with the butcher! Poor Jack, when daylight came he could hardly believe his eyes, there were no rabbits, not a single one, but he found the glass, and near each piece a neat round bullet-hole in the bank. The bullets had gone home alright, and so had the message. Neither of us spoke of this incident afterwards, but honour was satisfied, and the next night I received a matchbox full of empty shell cases, so Jack had recognised an equal adversary.

That first summer in Milton box was a happy one. On the night shift the work could be carried out in daylight almost the whole time, the hours of darkness were so short, and on the early and late shifts I began to learn about the intricacy of signal wire adjustment, to allow for temperature changes, the adjustments using those tall derrick-like contraptions standing behind the frame and coupled to the signals, each with its own winding gear slotted on to the long threaded spindle. On the early turn, as the sun began to climb and heat up, the sharp tang of creosoted sleepers would waft up and into the box, and the rails would begin to 'whang' as they expanded, and that was a sure sign of a lot of work ahead. The wire would begin to sag between the pulleys and the signals would not respond to the lever movements, so it would be time to start winding in the slack, turning the winder on the derricks perhaps fifty times before the signals would begin operating again. Before long, a cloud might pass over, and the slack would have to be let out again, and this would go on all day, winding in and out, an additional chore to the normal box working. Points were not affected by this expansion because the blades were not coupled and so had a 'run off' but the locking bars to the points were very prone to give trouble because the signal detector blades that passed through the locking bars would expand at the wire end and would not engage in the slotted blade. Although the points could be changed they could not be locked, but as with most problems, this could be overcome without much trouble, with a little bit of knowledge not shown in the rule book. It was a way out without affecting safety standards or delaying the trains, and it was all done with a little bit of wood, in fact, a matchstick. The first indication that the heat had caused expansion was when the points were changed, and it was found that the locking bar would not go in, which meant that the signal could not be pulled off, so the signalman would go down the stairs to the affected point with a box of matches. All locking bar detector blades are drilled with a series of holes so that the signal linesman can take up any adjustment necessary, so it was possible to pull back the blade, by hand, until one of these holes cleared the locking slot, and then the matchstick could be inserted in the hole and the blade eased back on the stop, the matchstick being just strong enough to hold it there. Then came a quick dash back up into the signal box, to change points, and push home the locking bar, breaking the matchstick in the process, and off came the signals.

That little dodge helped us out of heavy delays very often until the repairs could be done, but it was only possible, of course, where the points were close to the box. If they were some way away, then it was sometimes possible to clear the defect by slamming over the points in the hope that the detector could be jumped in, and if that didn't work, then trains would have to stop at that signal until the signal linesman came and attended to it, and, in fairness to them, they were a good lot of lads, turning out at once on receipt of a telephone call.

As with all kinds of transport it was not so much the traffic that became a problem, but the weather. Fog meant delays, gales would blow out signal lamps, snow would block points and freeze signals and cover up the signal glass, and thunderstorms would discharge electricity and affect all the signal box circuits, and my first experience of a thunderstorm was very spectacular. At eight in the evening as I had the last look round my garden, the atmosphere began to get heavy and the sinking sun had a copper tint about it. When I left home at half past nine there was a dullness on the horizon, not the sort of evening to leave my wife alone, but I had to go to work and hope that she would be all right. In the Swindon direction a blackness was beginning to sweep across the sky, and outside the quietness was unbelievable, the birds had stopped their twittering, there was no gentle evening breeze, everything was deathly still. I rang Highworth Junction, and my worst fears were confirmed, because they were in the middle of a severe thunderstorm, and it was creeping up the line towards me.

I had all the windows of the box open to allow what little air there was to circulate, and I stood at the open window and watched the 9.40p.m. parcels train from Swindon pass on the Up main line, the locomotive gleaming, the paint washed clean, and water cascading from the van gutters, and yet there was no rain here, just this dry stillness. The driver and fireman pointed back towards Steventon, and now I could see that the darkness was speeding towards me, a solid blanket of heavy cloud rumbling with anger.

The parcels train swept on towards Foxhall, its tail lamp light dancing and flickering on the last vehicle. I began placing the signals back, then went to the shelf and knocked out on the block bell 'train out of section' and as I did so, a great blast of wind came roaring through, sending notices flying off the hooks on the wall. Long-forgotten ash came billowing out from under the stove, and the trees opposite bowed towards the east, the leaves stripped off altogether in that great powerful draught. Then equally suddenly, came the rain, not a steady rain, but a great slamming deluge pouring out of that heavy cloud as a solid wall of water advanced up the line. It hit the side of the box with the open window, and drove a sharp distinct line across the polished floor, so I ran over to shut the window, and keep out the tempest. As the Down freight passed I could see the visible effort being made by the locomotive punching its way forward and saw the driver and fireman squeezed up in the corner as they tried to obtain some protection. Although I had never been in such a storm as this one, I could well remember what it had been like on the footplate, with the rain whipping past the cab, hissing and spitting where the suction from the firebox drew it in to hit the hot firebox flap, and the lightning striking the wet rails a mile ahead and racing up the line. Even so, I was not prepared for such fury as the storm was about to release.

When the first strike of lightning came, it was with a jagged whipcrack of angry red flame, ripping down from the black cloud to strike into the field opposite, lighting up the whole area for a split second, the trees and signal posts standing out stark in that sudden blinding flash, while the stench of sulphur filled the box. Immediately there was a colossal crack of thunder directly overhead, obliterating the clanging of all the block bells and telephones, and I was plunged into darkness. The sudden discharge of all that electricity activated every bit of box equipment as I groped my way over to the locker, found the hand lamp and lit it. I lifted down the emergency oil lamps with tall chimneys, only to find them covered in dust and empty, the wicks dry and unused, which did not help the situation.

I now had another lesson to learn in signal box work, how to decipher block bell codes from the constant jungle of interference caused by each lightning strike, and how to pull off signals and book trains in the register, with the aid of only one hand lamp. It was half an hour before I managed to fill the empty lamps with oil and re-hang them from the ceiling, in between scrabbling round dealing with trains. Once they were hung and lit, I made up my mind that I would never be caught out again, realising that those lamps were there for an emergency such as this, and in future, they would always be ready for use.

As the storm raged, we had to resort to the telephone instead of block bells, because it was quite impossible to understand any kind of bell code, with the constant interference from the lightning making the bells ring continually. I also came across another phenomenon new to me, as the electrical discharge built up in the air, so did the static, and it was transformed into St. Elmo's Fire, dancing and flickering along the top of the shining signal levers. I had been told to expect this during a thunderstorm, and I had also been told that because of the excellent earthing

Enjoying a day out, with a difference, on the Bluebell Railway on August 31st 1980. *Author*

My home shed. This fine photograph shows the rebuilding of the new shed. *British Rail*

Didcot Foxhall Junction Box, just as it was completed. *British Rail*

Immaculate as usual, inside the Foxhall Junction Box. Notice the duster over the lever. *British Rail*

View from the window of Didcot West Box, with the Oxford lines going to the left of the picture. *British Rail*

Coaling plant as new in Didcot shed, with the Provender Building in the right-hand distance. *British Rail*

My first signalbox, Milton 1950. A solid brick construction, but now, alas, only the base is left! *Author*

Aerial view of Culham Airfield. The railway is running adjacent to the perimeter (top left of photograph). *Author*

A Sea Fury landing behind Culham Signalbox. *Author*

Another interesting view as B52 bombers prepare to take-off behind Carterton Signalbox, on the Fairford Branch. *Author*

Disaster! *Polar Star*, No. 70026, laying at rest at the bottom of the embankment, after the Milton accident.   *British Rail*

A front view of the engine showing the lengths of rails clamped to the wheels prior to righting the engine.   *British Rail*

Block and tackle fixed to the locomotive ready for the 'big pull'. Note the
temporary track laid to haul the loco into the Milton Depot.   *British Rail*

She's up!   *British Rail*

View of the damaged side. *British Rail*

No. 3212 was used to pull out the unfortunate loco. Note the temporary packing on the track work. *British Rail*

Two of my favourite stations on the Didcot — Newbury line. The top photograph shows Compton with a three coach stopping train approaching the station with No. 30117 in charge. The lower photograph shows Hampstead Norris, a station with many memories for me.   *OPC Collection*

My favourite engine, *City of Truro*, with a special waiting at Churn station. The unusual island platform and shelter did not help in the cold winter months.

OPC Collection

No. 3212 with a goods train sweeping round the curve at Pinewood Halt.

OPC Collection

No. 7311 takes up ploughing at Appleford in September 1952. *Author*

The aftermath of No. 7311. All that's left of Appleford Signalbox in September 1952. *Author*

Bill Checkley, District Inspector, bottom left, surveys the damage of the accident. *Author*

Another two stations on the Southern Section of the Didcot, Newbury and Southampton Railway. Top photograph shows Sutton Scotney and the lower No. 3212 standing in Winchester Chesil Station, just after leaving the tunnel.

OPC Collection

Didcot North Junction as I remember it. Notice the trees painted on the signal box and building alongside. A wartime measure. *British Rail*

Wolvercote Junction box, north of Oxford with a freight train waiting to come off the Worcester Main line. *British Rail*

Three local signal boxes
around Oxford.
Top Hinksey North
Middle Morris Cowley
Lower Oxford Station
South

A mixed freight train going through Taplow with No. 5326 in charge.

N.H.A. Shelton

The end of the line! Paddington with its fine overall roof. Always a restful place for me!

N.E. Stead

Waiting to depart from Horsted Keynes in August 1980. *Author*

Footplate colleagues at Didcot in 1948. Driver Bill Trubey (seated), driver Bert Johns (behind), fireman John Bennetts (right), fireman John Smith (left).

Author

The man who made it all possible, my 'old chap', Harold Gasson Senior. *Author*

properties of a signal box, it was one of the safest of places to be, but nevertheless it took some courage on my part to handle those levers. That storm became trapped inside the Thames Valley, rolling and rumbling round until two in the morning. In one brief instant during a particularly bad lightning flash, I can remember glancing out of the rear window across Milton depot and seeing very clearly the white lines of a church tower miles away across the countryside. Later in the week in daylight, I had a look through a small telescope, and realised that what I had seen during the storm was the tower of the chapel attached to Culham College, a lovely view not possible today, because, in the way, stands the giant Didcot Power Station, on the site of the depot.

For a Class Three main line signal box, Milton would take some beating for a newcomer to be weaned on, as it was new and modern, it had running water and a wash-basin inside, large windows for a perfect all-round view, and a flush toilet inside in the frame room. Every kind of traffic was dealt with, from light engines to the expresses and the traffic was heavy enough to keep one busy, yet light enough to enable one to enjoy a cup of tea and a sandwich between trains. It was gentle going compared with some boxes, there was time to study the rules and regulations and hold quizzes with the other lads on the phone, each of us trying hard to catch out the other chap, and without realising it at the time, I was soaking up all this knowledge until the time came when I was able to give as good as I got, and I felt that I was now right on top of this job.

The time came round for the yearly examination by the District Inspector, which was not a sudden spot check; we all knew that he was on the trail after he had visited the first box, because the news went through the district at once. So I was not surprised when one day I saw Bill Checkley come cycling down the path towards me, a Relief signalman trailing along behind him ready to take over my duties while Bill put me through the rules and regulations. Soon he was at me, to the background of bells, lever movements, and trains rattling past, not an ideal situation to sit an examination, but that was the way it was done in those days. Bill was never the one to ask the odd question, he started at the beginning of the book and worked his way through, missing nothing, headlamp codes, bell codes, emergencies, standard block, permissive block, fog working, single line working, and station limits, and although we were in a main line situation at Milton, he even included questions on working a single line with tokens.

While the District Inspector was downstairs in the toilet, the Relief signalman confided in me that Bill had given me the hardest examination so far, he still was a little bit wary of this ex-footplate man in one of his boxes, the average session was only half an hour, and yet I had been ploughing through for an hour. Thank goodness I had got through without any trouble, as the Relief signalman had been sweating on some of those questions, because if I had fumbled on any, Bill would have expected him to give the correct reply, being a senior man. However, that long session was to stand me in good stead in a couple of years, and went on my record, and to Bill's credit, in future examinations he never again put me through the hoop like that.

The summer service came to an end and the new winter time-tables gave a much reduced service on the passenger side, so now the traffic ought to drop off a bit, or so we all thought, but the increase in freight trains gave us plenty to do. With the football season in full swing, the special notices became thicker, and as each cup round was played, so the number of specials began to increase. They would begin in the early mornings each Saturday, Cardiffs, Swanseas, Bristols, Arsenals and Evertons, all flying about the system, and one weekend it came to a head with such volume as will probably never be seen again. Cardiff and Bristol were in a cup replay with two of the London clubs, and Swansea playing a league game, Wales were playing at Twickenham, and to top that lot, the American evangelist, Billy Graham, was holding a meeting in the Albert Hall. I knew that the Welsh nation had a liking for football and were known to be partial to a little rugby now and again, and that the remainder would turn up for a bit of Bible-thumping, providing that there was a small portion of the time set aside for some singing, but I had no idea what the mass evacuation of an entire nation could be like until that Saturday.

The whole freight programme was cancelled that weekend, and all those signal boxes such as Milton, which were normally closed on Sunday mornings, were booked to remain open, and each man on every shift throughout that weekend, worked as he had never worked before. The football and rugby specials started in the early morning, by five o'clock the first were going through, one behind the other, clearing by eight o'clock for the normal passenger service, then in the afternoon the Billy Graham specials began to follow on, mixed up with the afternoon and evening expresses, the train register on the Up side page showing row upon row of 'A' headcodes. The locomotive power for all these trains was something to see, 'Castles', 'Halls', 'Granges', 'Manors', and battered old 'forty-threes' that had not been at the head of a passenger train for years, let alone pulling an express, and each batch of specials dropped down the range of locomotives as the shed foremen scratched around for suitable power. Even two of the 'forty-seven' class, not normally used in the winter because of the lack of steam heating, were pressed into service, and one train towards the end of this mass exodus was headed by a grand old lady, a 'twenty-eight', her side-rods flashing round with the steam as it whipped back from her safety valve giving the impression that she was flying by at eighty instead of fifty, whilst the fireman leaned out of the cab with the slack of the coal-watering pipe in his hand, beating the side of the cab with it, urging her on, just like a jockey nearing the finishing post. When they were all gone, the Up main line was cleared for the delayed freights to run, and they too were one behind the other, hour after hour, at the expense of the Down traffic, which had, in turn, been held back, because just as the last Up special arrived at Paddington, the first of the returns began. Football specials started hammering away for home, dripping with paper streamers, and passengers littering the countryside with empty beer bottles and seat cushions. After these were gone, the Albert Hall returns began, lasting until the early hours, running so tightly behind each other, that it was rare for any of them to see a distant signal off in its favour, but these were quiet trains, with compartments full of sleeping people, as they were hurried back to the valleys.

It took a week for the normal freight traffic to recover from that weekend, and for days afterwards, engines were running light back from South Wales to their home sheds. One aspect of my signalman's job I did enjoy, was the first-hand view that I had of locomotive testing. Weeks beforehand, we received the special notice and the timings for this programme and when it came it was well worth waiting for; to the other lads it was, admittedly, something out of the ordinary, and a little bit interesting, but to me it was real meat and drink.

It started with 6001 *King Edward VII* running up from Stoke Gifford to Reading with the dynamometer coach and twenty-five coaches tied on behind running at 60mph, and when that engine stuck her nose under Steventon bridge coming towards me, I could hardly believe my eyes. It looked as if there was the side of a garden shed stuck on the front, and, as she drew near, I could see that there was indeed a wooden shelter built on to the front frame and nailed back to the smoke box, with two little round windows let in at each side. Amazingly, there were people in there, because I could see two faces peering through the glass, but what it could have been like in there I can only imagine, as the roar from that chimney was like a volcano. The engine passed with the footplate full of people, then line after line of coaches, it was the longest passenger stock train that I had ever seen.

The trials went on for several weeks using other engines, all with these great loads. No. 1000 *County of Middlesex* was one to be hammered up through the section, then came No. 1009 *County of Carmarthen* now sporting a horrible little stove-pipe chimney, but the end of these trials was achieved with a run that was most interesting. In April, No. 6003 *King George IV* ran a test train from Paddington to Bristol with only eight coaches on, leaving Paddington at 10.55 a.m. and passing me at Milton at 12.03 p.m. going all out, so that she was through Steventon bridge before I could put all the signals back and past Steventon box in one minute, halving the normal express passenger time; this was the prototype Bristolian giving us a taste of things to come.

The next lot of tests that came my way were a bit of a shock to me, as I was used to the clean lines of the Great Western locomotive. That was when the first of the 'Britannias' came on the scene, great big powerful brutish-looking engines, running through with twenty-odd coaches on, and when they did take over regular services, it was to knock the beautiful 'Castles' out of the picture. One train, the Red Dragon up from Cardiff, was always run with a 'Castle' from Canton shed, a shed that took a pride in turning out the locomotive in showroom condition, but one Monday morning the train came up with a new 'Britannia', and we never saw the 'Castles' again on this train, but, to be fair to the new class of engine, they kept time, even if they did seem to be working hard at it.

The sequel was the introduction of the ten-wheel coupled 9Fs, and on the first test, this ugly locomotive came exploding through the bridge, tearing towards me, the exhaust climbing into the sky in a tall column before spreading out over the twenty-six coaches behind. Between the Down starting signal and my Up home signal the special brake test took place. The exhaust was cut off instantly to be replaced by the roar of steam from the safety valves and I could see smoke pouring out from the wheels as the brake blocks bit into the tyres, then the coaches began to shudder and they disappeared in a cloud of dirty brown rust, as all the accumulated rust and dirt was shaken out from under the frames.

They stopped for the booked five minutes at my home signal, people in white overalls swarmed out of the dynamometer car to look round the engine and the train. I could hear the ejector roaring up through the chimney, fighting to release the vacuum brakes, then the train began to move forward, the engine working hard to drag all those coaches against some of the brake blocks which were reluctant to free from the wheels. As the engine passed me, I looked down into the cab, the air in the box whistling past as it was sucked out by the displacement of the engine exhaust, rattling the windows in their window-frames with each beat from the chimney. As the engine began to get to grips with that load, the driver pulled back on the regulator giving her more steam, then looked up at me and grinned, pointing over his shoulder towards the inside of the cab. I nodded my head and grinned back, to see two firemen, stripped to the waist, both as black as any coal miner, one opening and closing the fire hole doors, the other shovelling the coal in. No wonder lads were leaving the service, that was not just work, it was hard labour, without the benefit of having committed any crime.

It took that train as long as any goods train to clear the section, but there was no doubt as to what I had seen, those 9Fs might be freight locomotives and perhaps replacements for the ageing twenty-eights, but they were certainly capable of running a passenger train too. I never had the chance to fire or drive one, or indeed to go on the footplate while they were in service, but when *Evening Star* arrived for preservation at the Great Western Society's depot in my old shed at Didcot, I had a look round the engine, and a good long hard look on the footplate, and as an ex-locomotive man, I could appreciate what a fine locomotive this was.

Chapter Four

Promotion

When promotion came, it was far in excess of what I had expected. My three years at Milton had been happy ones, but they had made me very used to routine; twenty-five minutes to get to work, cover the duty, then twenty-five minutes back home again, day after day. I was now conditioned to a sedentary job, and expecting to obtain promotion one day, into one of the bigger local boxes, but in the back of my mind I still missed the open road that I had enjoyed in the Locomotive Department. Then, out of the blue, there came a change in the working conditions, when the basic week of 48 hours was reduced to 44 hours. This caused some complications because we were all working an eight hour day for a 48 hour week, so implementation of the new arrangement took some working out. The difficulty was surmounted by both the management and unions agreeing to an 88-hour fortnight, and introducing a 'rest day' every other week, but before anyone could have this day off, there had to be someone to cover the duty. There were not enough Relief men to do it, as they were only intended to cover holidays and sickness, so a new grade was created, Rest Day Relief Signalman.

I didn't stand a chance of this new job, as there were dozens of class two men far ahead of me, and it took years to become a relief man because it was the top job, equal to that of a top link engine driver, but I stood a fair chance of getting into a class two box to replace one of those men if they went into relief work. The notice came round inviting signalmen to apply for one of the new posts, it was advertised as Rest Day Relief as distinct from the normal Relief man, and to my surprise, it was a class one job. We all put in applications for these positions, as it was not often a class one came on the market. The management were in a hurry, being bound by the agreement to implement this reduction of hours as quickly as possible. When I pushed my application through Bill Checkley's letter-box, I knew full well, that as a class three man with only three years of service in a signal box I stood little chance of being considered for the new grade. Within a week I received acknowledgement of my application from the District

Operating Superintendent's office at Paddington, and a week later to the day, I received the following letter:

'List No. 45 Vacancy No. 1769 District Relief Signalman Cl.1 Didcot (mainly Rest Day Relief)

I am pleased to inform you that you have been approved for the above vacancy with effect from 31.1.52, subject to competency not being delayed beyond a reasonable period of training.

I will advise you later regarding date of transfer.

Will you please note'

Would I please note! I would indeed, I could hardly believe it, and I still have that memo along with my other bits of railway history. The next letter was from Bill Checkley and it read:

'In connection with the above will you please commence learning duties as from Monday next 28th inst, reporting to this office after taking rest'.

I finished my last shift at Milton on the Saturday, clearing out my locker with a feeling of sadness. Again I was filled with the same doubts as three years previously when I had left the footplate, whether I had bitten off more than I could chew, and I wondered how my application had come to be approved. The answer to that question came when I reported to Bill Checkley on the Monday morning, because both he and Freddie Blackhall had recommended me.

That Monday, I was in a bit of a dream. I spent the day at Didcot West End, filling in time really, because I was booked to go to Paddington the next day, travelling on the familiar train, the 7.05 a.m, to visit Chief Inspector Honeybone, but this time without the worry and concern of the previous visit, although I did have a few 'butterflies in the tummy' nevertheless.

This time there was no messing about, and I didn't end up in the Board Room, but went straight into the little outer office, and finding it empty, I knocked on the door of the inner office and walked in. Inspector Honeybone was on the telephone, so he gestured to me to sit down. Whoever was on the other end was receiving a real rocket, and I began to have some doubts, as I really didn't want this particular gentleman to be upset today, but I need not have worried. When he put the phone down, he shook hands and said how pleased he was to see me. He had been through my record, and he had no intention of giving me questions on rules to answer, and this visit was a formality, just to say that he had seen me, and that he thought I was suitable to take up relief work.

There was then another handshake and I was outside again, down on the familiar platform with honking taxis, echoing tannoys, and the bustling background that makes up Paddington station.

I was back at Didcot by 10.40 a.m. reporting to Bill Checkley, and feeling very pleased with life, to think that I had made a top job in just three years, and I had a head start with it, having an intimate knowledge of the box at Milton. What the future would bring, I didn't know, but I would cross that bridge when I came to it.

Bill and Freddie were struggling, trying to work out a roster to give every signalman, including the relief men, a day off once a fortnight, and as there were 72 of them altogether, they were having a right old headache. They were also trying to find time for the new men such as myself to learn a big district, but Bill did have a job for me, and asked me to go and cover the vacancy at Milton until he could release me. As he gently pointed out, I would be covering my old job, so within two days I was back there, and likely to be so for a few weeks, so I opened up my locker again and settled in, but this time, I was on a higher rate of pay. I was also being paid walking time from Didcot, twenty minutes to the mile, two miles each way, which made an hour and a half extra each day, although in fact, I still rode my bike.

After two weeks covering my own vacancy, my replacement turned up. Granville Burt, one of the nicest chaps I have ever met, from Upton on the Newbury branch, was not a 'sprog' of a signalman, as I had been, but a chap with some service behind him, so we got on like a house on fire.

Granville was used to double line working (but not in any volume) but he had no experience with permissive block working with goods loops. To Granville, it seemed against all nature to allow two or more trains into the section on the same line, and as it happened, freight traffic was heavy at that time, and the goods loops were in full use, both Up and Down. I was therefore able to show him the procedure, of how to bring a train to a stand at the loop home signal, then allow it to pull forward, instruct the driver as to how many were in front, then obtain the permission from the box ahead to allow the train in and allow it to proceed. The one thing to be careful of, was, to turn the loop block indicator to the correct figure, either one, two or three, and to make sure that this figure was reduced when one of the trains cleared at the other end.

On the Down side, it was a bit difficult to shout across, so we would stand at the open window and show two or three fingers to

68

the driver. If he gave a toot on the whistle, then we knew he understood, but if he ignored our gesture, then he was stopped at the signal entering the loop, then allowed to pull forward, and he would then know that there was another train in front of him. This was quite a safe method of working, because the drivers and guards were all aware of the regulations regarding permissive block working, they too had to pass the examinations, and the only time the guard was involved was during fog or falling snow, then he had to go back behind his train and lay detonators on the line. During my time as a fireman, I had spent many hours with my driver blocked back in a loop behind other trains, and it was a very nice situation on a dirty night, to bank up the fire, fill the boiler, and then join the guard of the train in front in his warm guard's van.

Granville had three weeks with me, one week on each shift, and it gave me the opportunity to give him the help that I had received from Bert Vokings three years before. I even tried Bert's trick of clearing off down the line to Steventon, which was interesting for me, as I had worked with Arthur Stoner for three years and had got to know him well, and yet, he was just a voice on the telephone, and at last, I had a chance to meet him and have a look at his signal box.

On the Wednesday of the third week, Bill Checkley rang me and asked how Granville was getting on. I told Bill that I considered that he was ready to take over, so Bill got on his bike and came to put Granville through the hoop, but there was no problem there. While I ran the box, Granville answered every question on the rules that Bill threw at him, and I was pleased to sign my name on the certificate that gave him the key to go forward to Paddington. He went the next day, a bit worried about Chief Inspector Honeybone, but I had told him truthfully, that I had found this big man to be a gentleman, and when Granville returned the next day, it was with the news that he had passed and would be taking over on the following Monday. The wheel had turned full circle.

Bill Checkley sent me a letter giving me instructions for the following months, but before I had time to open it, he rang me and said he would like me to take my time learning the new boxes, but at the same time not to be too long about it, only to let him know when I was moving on to another box. I opened the letter after this conversation, and nearly fell through the floor. I had only seventeen weeks to cover the district in time for implementation of the new 44-hour week, and the list of boxes was given, Foxhall Junction, Appleford, Culham, Radley, Sandford,

Kennington Junction, Hinksey South, Wolvercote Sidings, Wolvercote Junction and Kidlington.

I made a start at Foxhall, simply because I knew the service and it was a box that I took to my heart. If ever a perfect junction box existed, then it must be Foxhall, there was all the main line running such as I had known at Milton, plus the goods loops, the West Curve traffic, traffic into and out of Didcot depot, and the sidings into the Provender Stores.

Foxhall was good basic training, because that list that I thought was so long grew to include Moreton Cutting and yard, Cholsey, Aston Tirrold, Didcot North Junction, Yarnton, Didcot West End, Nuneham, Abingdon, Hinksey North, Oxford Station South, Oxford North Junction, Witney, Carterton and Fairford, twenty-five boxes including Milton. I would have thought it impossible for any person to hold the knowledge of all those boxes under his hat, but it was possible, and there were some chaps who knew even more.

There were three first class chaps at Foxhall to choose from, Bill Ackrill, my original mate, Arthur Ryman and Jack Drew. I chose to go with Jack, not because he was any better than the others, but because he was the early turn man, and if I was going to spend the better part of three months learning the district, I might as well be on the day shift, there would be enough night and afternoon turns when we got cracking.

Jack made me welcome, so much so, I thought he must have forgotten about shooting at those bits of glass a couple of years back. He called out the lever numbers to me as I started to learn the frame, and I was gaining confidence as the trains ran by; that was his method, for him to call out the numbers while I pulled the levers, but then, on the last one, there was an almighty explosion under my feet. Flame and smoke shot up my trouser leg and I stood there trembling with shock until I realised that Jack had played one of his tricks on me. While I had been setting the road from the West Curve into the depot, Jack had been down in the frame room, and while there he wrapped the lead straps of a fog detonator round a spare lever so that when I pulled that lever, I rammed it up against the stop and exploded it.

I sat in the chair with my heart thumping like a 'King' going up Dainton bank, deciding that somehow I would have to think up another trick for Jack, and it would have to be something good, as he was an adversary to respect.

After three weeks at Foxhall, I felt that I could handle the box, so I moved on to Appleford and now that I came on to the Oxford branch telephone system, I found that there were two other relief signalmen about. Three of us had been appointed to cover the new work, and these other two chaps were working their way up from Oxford, one was Eddie Edwards who had given up Appleford to come on the relief staff, and the other was Ken Finch who had come from Wolvercote Junction. I was to find out later that Ken was actually better at leg-pulling than both Jack and me put together.

Appleford was a nice little box, just the Up and Down main line outside the box, then on the Didcot side a pair of facing points to turn Up goods trains in, and a Down goods loop to turn trains out. The box was built in the traditional Great Western manner with brickwork for the frame room and wood with a gabled roof for the operating part. Access was up a wooden stairway on the outside, the whole box being adjacent to the level crossing. The crossing was not a busy one, open only when the residents from Arkwright's farm needed to come across, or when Cyril Butterworth, the regular signalman who lived in the cottage behind the box, decided to get his car out, but with a level crossing it did make a change for me to be in close touch with the public.

The road ran, with a sweeping curve, from Didcot to the village opposite the box so there was always something going on. To obtain water, we would go to the cottage opposite and draw it from the well. Fred Tyler and his wife lived there, and Fred worked on the farm, but was retained by the railway to take care of the tilley lamps at Appleford Halt, so he was a frequent visitor to the box. I spent a week there, which was enough to learn that box, then I moved on to Culham, a little old-fashioned box tucked up against a low bank, due to be demolished as soon as the new box on the platform was ready. One day there sufficed, as I had spent hours in this box unofficially when I had first begun thinking about transferring from the footplate. The next day I moved to Radley where I spent two weeks in the company of Wally Turner, who had been at the Reading Signal School with me. Radley was an interesting place, where the box was on the platform, so we were always in the public eye, and we had the company of the porters and the station master, plus a new type of signalling to me, the Abingdon single line branch.

I was beginning to enjoy myself, coming and going to work by train, but the further from Didcot I progressed the longer between home it took, and for the next box at Sandford meant I had to take my bike with me. I was to find when I began to 'work the district' that bike rides would average out at a hundred miles each week. Sandford I found to be like Milton, two main lines with an Up and Down goods loop, except that the Oxford side between Kennington Junction and Sandford was an Up Relief, reverting to a goods loop on the Didcot side of the box. There was a lead into the Kennington cold store from the Down loop, but it was not used very often. I found that a week was quite enough here, not only because it was so like Milton but because right behind the box the Sandford sewerage plant was situated, and after eight hours on duty it was the fresh air that smelt queer when I left!

My next box was Kennington Junction, and here I briefly met Ken and Eddie working their way south. We were at the halfway mark, and soon we would be getting together to work the district. My tutor at Kennington was a little Scot, Bob Chalmers, and what a help he proved to be. He would come on duty frozen after riding a little motor cycle all the way from Chilton on the Berkshire Downs, and he was looking forward to moving into a new house in the near future, which gave me an idea; Kennington was right in the middle of my district, how nice it would be to live there also. Bob, bless him, introduced me to the local councillor whose garden backed on to the goods loop behind the box, and he told me that a programme had just been passed to build a new estate a mile up the line towards Sandford, and I ought to get my name on the list. I did this straight away, and within a year I had a home and had moved in.

Kennington was the classic junction box from the old broad gauge days, very tall, and perched right in the middle of the Up and Down main line with the junction sweeping down from the Princes Risborough branch to join the main line in front of the box. It was not long before the Oxford drivers and firemen found me there, and they knew that I was an old footplate man used to catching single line tokens at speed, and although the normal arrangement was to throw the hoop onto the catcher which was some way from the box, if they saw me leaning out of the end window, they would come roaring down off that branch at forty miles an hour, knowing that I would catch the token, and save myself a walk. Two weeks at Kennington and a telephone call to Bill Checkley confirmed that I was keeping up with the other two lads and running to the estimated training time. I had only four more boxes to go, and Hinksey South came next, another of the brick and flat-roofed war time boxes, much bigger than Milton, with the addition of a great big goods yard to contend with. I spent three weeks there, knowing that I could afford the time if I reduced the duties at the next box. I found that I was picking up the working of all these boxes better than I had thought I would, and that was because of the advice one of the senior relief men had given me, which was simply to write down in a little book the numbers of the lever movements. That little book was to be invaluable when I started the circuit.

Leaving Hinksey South, the list omitted the Oxford boxes and picked up again at Wolvercote Sidings, just a small passing box which I mastered in one day. Wolvercote Junction proved to be quite a surprise, it was as busy as Foxhall, dealing with all of the Banbury traffic and that of the 'Old Worse and Worry' line together with Yarnton goods yard and the Fairford branch. I spent a good three weeks there before moving to the last box at Kidlington for a couple of days, and ended up the week all ready to go into action the following week. I had never known time to fly so, seventeen weeks after leaving Milton I now knew the workings of nine other signal boxes, and had been introduced to many different kinds of signal equipment. My head was filled to bursting point with all the differing details I had had to learn, so that looking back now, years later, I wonder how any of us managed to handle it, perhaps because we were younger then and better able to cope.

I was the first to kick off (it has always seemed in my life that I am chosen to be the first) and I started on this two week cycle at Milton; no problems there back in my old box, and it was nice to fall into the pattern of a service that I was brought up on, and on my old regular turn, so that I was working with my original mates again, but I did have Foxhall Junction to face tomorrow, and it had been seventeen weeks since I had learnt that box. That Tuesday morning I relieved Jack Drew, and before going up into the box, I checked the frame for fog detonators, not wanting to get caught twice. I checked the saddle bag on his bike, yes, he was still carrying round the half hundred weight of old fish plate bolts that I had placed in there all those weeks ago, and I would soon have to do something about fixing him in a proper manner!

I had a sick feeling in my stomach as I took over from him, and watched him cycle up the path for home, wishing that he could have stopped for an hour while I played myself in. The block bells began to ring, demanding attention, and I got down to work, Up main, Down Main, a trip into the depot followed by the work-men's passenger train from Oxford, a couple of Southern engines down from Moreton yard to turn, sending them round the West Curve to North Junction, and by the time I looked round, two hours had passed, the register was booked up to date, and I had a clear block, with no trains piled up in a heap outside, so I realised that I was winning, and began to enjoy myself. At nine the Up fasts began to appear, the 7.00a.m. Weston followed by the Fishguard, the slip coach dropping anchor just before reaching the box, then came the Cheltenham and the Swansea with the Bristol on her heels, and so tight behind, the Weston slipped right outside the box after I had given her a distant signal check. I could see the coupling drop away, and the vacuum and steam pipes part. She should not really have slipped with the distant on, as it was against the rules, although I had cleared it about a coach length behind. My old uncle, Bert Edmunds, loved this train and, as he was one of the top link drivers at Old Oak Common, I would now be seeing him in action, and he never slipped at Didcot with the Weston unless he was over the ninety mark. That duty passed quickly, it seemed no time at all when Ken Finch came into the box to relieve me, but I left him to it, tired after so much concentration, knowing that tomorrow would be spent at Appleford, which was as good as a day off. I never looked back after that first duty at Foxhall, I had broken the ice, and I could now settle down.

As the months rolled by, the job became routine. We would relieve each other early if that meant a train home could be caught, or stop on if it meant our mate being able to come by train instead of a long cycle ride. If a 20-mile ride was unavoid-able, as it very often was, first-hand information about road conditions was important, since in the winter, snow-drifts were commonplace, and also floods. We were up at 3.00a.m. leaving home at four to cycle twenty or more miles to be on duty at six, always sure in the knowledge that when we got there the fire would be burning brightly and a pot of tea would be on the table. The only gripe that we had was that we could bike all those miles in some of the worst weather this old country was capable of throwing, and be there on time, and yet, some of the regular signalmen who would be relieving the night relief man (and who lived so close we could see their homes) would be late, turning up perhaps ten minutes behind time, and often losing us a train home.

As we worked together we became close friends, and familiarity brought the fun, between Ken Finch and myself anyway. Eddie

Edwards, although a very nice chap, was a bit less exuberant, but being an ex-Appleford man, he did introduce us to the farmer's wife, Mrs. Arkwright, which in turn brought us into the market for eggs, not the shop eggs stamped with a little lion, but big rich old-fashioned brown eggs with some real flavour.

One week when I was at Appleford I had a most exciting time. I had collected my eggs, when the good lady came over the crossing in her car taking the children to school, and I had beaten Fred Tyler's dog between the well and the gate without spilling any of my water, no mean feat to outrun a cross bred greyhound. Fred Tyler, who was ploughing the field opposite, gave a shout and stopped the tractor, so I placed the water can on the crossing on the safe side of the fence away from that dog, and crossed the road into the field. Fred was scraping the mud from an object which looked, at first glance, like an unexploded bomb, but as the mud cleared, it began to take shape and we saw it was a mass of hundreds of Roman coins stuck together. All but two of these coins ended up in the Ashmolean Museum in Oxford, but Fred had one and I had the other, in fact, I still have it. The newspaper report said that the coins were 1,600 years old, and came from the period of Constantine the Great. To think they had lain in that field all that time just for Fred and me to pick up.

Apart from their care of the Halt lamps, Fred and his wife were thought a great deal of by the railway people, because some years previously when the Down Birkenhead express had hit the wreckage of a derailment outside the box, the first coach had sheared across the Up main and ploughed through their garden landing up against the front door, and they were both soon out of bed and giving help to the injured. They both, in a way, were adopted railway folk, and later, when a similar accident happened, they were the first on the scene with help.

It was while I was at Appleford for the day, that I found out how kind and considerate Ken Finch was. I relieved him early on the afternoon shift so that he could cycle down the line to Culham and catch the train back home to Oxford, and as he left the box, he mentioned that there were 50 young brussels sprouts plants up in the corner for me, carefully wrapped in newspaper and soaking in a bucket of water. I gave 25 to Eddie Edwards when he relieved me at 10.00p.m. and the next morning with all the enthusiasm of a trainee gardener, I planted mine out, but this was to be a long-term joke of Ken's. Those plants just grew and grew, they turned into the finest patch of cow kale ever seen, with stalks as thick as trees, and eventually, I had to use an axe to cut them down.

When we took over Culham, it was to be in the new box, which had been built on the Oxford end of the Up platform, so we were in the public eye, and the windows were so low that people could look into the box, but it was a nice duty there, working with the porters and the Station Master for company. Culham was an interesting place, between the box and the bridge on the Oxford side and to the east of the cutting was an airfield, a Fleet Air Arm branch of the service, H.M.S. Hornbill, flying Sea Furies of 1832 Squadron, and within a few weeks they began to change over to Vampires. It was quite a racket to hear the banshee wail of a jet engine as they took off and landed, after being used to the Rolls Merlins of the Sea Furies. The flight path was right over the main line, so we had a crash bell fitted in the box, and a telephone so we were in direct contact with the control tower on the airfield in case of emergency.

I only had one emergency while I was there, and that did not affect the main line. I watched the pilot come in with a Vampire, side-slipping as he flared in, and he clipped the fence with his under-carriage, leaving a couple of wheels behind and an ugly column of black smoke drifting back over the railway. That telephone was mostly used by the lads on the airfield, when they enquired about train times, which was very handy, as they would ring up to see how the afternoon Up stopper was running (it connected at Didcot with the London train), then half a dozen of them would come over the fence, scrabbling down the bank, and underneath the box, dressed like sailors going in, but civilians coming out as the train ran into the station. At the last minute, when the guard was blowing his whistle, they would dash out and into the train. Time after time, just as the train cleared the platform, two beefy perspiring, angry-looking pickets with red armbands and white gaiters would run onto the platform, and they always asked us if we had seen any sailors get on the train, but the answer they got was always true, only civilians had boarded the train. This procedure was reversed later in the evening when the lads returned, and we never split on them, perhaps because of the carton of duty-free cigarettes left behind for understanding signalmen. Culham was full of fun, and we got on well with the porters. One of them was an old chap and he was fascinated by the new jet aircraft, so, with a straight face, I happened to mention that the 5.00 p.m. stopper up from Oxford had some canisters of compressed smoke on board for these jet engines. When the train ran in, that dear old chap carefully unloaded two large cylinders of welding oxy-acetylene that just happened to be for the airfield and dragged them on a station trolley all the way round to the airfield stores, but after this leg-pull, he soon learnt to be wary of Ken and myself.

We had an anxious moment one day, when the Government were clearing out a dump of army vehicles at Dorchester, and these vehicles were loaded into wagons that had been shunted into the cattle sidings behind the signal box. It used to break our hearts to see dozens of motor-cycles tipped into those wagons, all upside down with the handle bars of some rammed through the spokes of the wheels of those underneath, while we had to ride push-bikes just because we couldn't afford to buy a motor-cycle. On this day, however, there were Low-Loaders shunted in, and they had been loaded with lorries, all except one which contained a Bedford lorry, but the rear end had been converted to hold a mobile crane. I relieved Ken who stopped behind for a few minutes for the Down train to take him home, so being nosy, we stepped from the platform and on to the floor bed of the Low-Loader to have a look at this interesting vehicle. The crane was coupled up to a diesel engine, independent of the engine of the vehicle, and there was an impressive panel bolted to the side, full of switches and dials, and right in the middle was just one button. As everyone knows, a button is there to be pressed, so we pressed it; there was a snort and a cough, and that blessed diesel engine began to run, settling down to turn over with a very soft 'chug, chug'.

Ken's train ran in, so he left me, and after I had dealt with the train and the block was clear, I tried everything to stop that engine. I pulled down switches, and even kicked it, but it wouldn't stop, it just kept on chugging away. At about four in the afternoon, Mr. Fouracre, the Station Master, came up into the box for a chat and a cup of tea. He sat there looking out of the window, and said, in casual conversation, that he could have sworn that he had seen the jib of that crane move. I had a look, and with a great deal of earnest effort, managed to persuade him that it was a distortion in the glass. That diesel ran all day and night, luckily stopping the next morning when the fuel ran out.

It was well known that Mr. Fouracre, the Station Master, was a bird-watcher, the feathered kind, of course, and the old broad gauge goods shed opposite the signal box was a haven for swallows, so there was nothing unusual in Mr. Fouracre propping up a ladder against the great oak beams that spanned the shed and settling down to watch for a couple of hours. I relieved Ken one afternoon, and off he went home. At four in the afternoon Mrs. Fouracre came over to the station, and made enquiries about her husband, as he hadn't come home for his dinner. Together we searched the area, and eventually we heard him shouting for help. He was perched up in the goods shed, legs straddling a beam, and the ladder miles away from where he had placed it, for Ken had nipped in and moved it! Mr. Fouracre was too much of a gentleman to take any official action over that, he could give as good as he got, and there would be another time for him to get his own back on Ken. There was, weeks later; he rang Ken up when he was at Radley, and putting on a voice very much like Bill Checkley, he asked for a complete list of all train bookings to be copied out of the train register, and sent to the District Inspector's Office, with a covering report of all shunting movements. Ken duly carried out this request, and sent it in, and Bill Checkley rang him up and said that one swallow does not make a summer, so Ken conceded that he had been rumbled.

Now all this might make the reader feel that signal box work was one long period of hilarity, but that was not the case, it was a rough, tough job and a responsible one to be carried out by young men like myself in their twenties. There had to be some relief in the normal working day or we would have gone mad. When the pressure was on, we were not lacking, we had a safety record to be proud of, but normal working is boring, and does not make good reading, so it is of the funny or unusual incidents in my railway career that I write about.

The next box down the line was Radley, which, like Culham, squatted on the Up platform, but with the Abingdon branch to add to the working. Once the little tank engine of the Abingdon branch had arrived from Oxford we did not have much to do with it, the branch was worked as a single line with one engine in steam, so once the single line staff was handed over, it was just a matter of it running back and forth, connecting with the various passenger trains that stopped at Radley.

By this time, Ken and I had become known as the 'terrible twins' but at least we did bring some life into the district. Bill Prior at Appleford added the spice with one incident, he pulled off a classic that is still talked about today wherever old signalmen gather together, and he managed it simply because he was a champion gardener. We were all linked up on the phone one afternoon in between trains talking about gardening, then Bill began to talk about a giant marrow which he had grown, feeding it on sugar water and beer. As a result, it had grown so big that he would have to borrow a hand cart from the farmer to move it, and he went on to say that a well-known firm who made soups was going to buy it from him for an advertisement. We took all this in, so much so, that the lad in Oxford Station South signal box called in at the *Oxford Mail* offices on the way home from work, thinking that it would make a news story, and they thought so too, and they sent a reporter and a photographer out to Appleford to see this wonderful marrow. Bill only got out of that one by convincing them that the marrow had already been collected by the soup firm, and telling them that there was far more going on at Radley, they ought to go there and interview the ghost.

Mr. Wright, the Station Master, believed in the ghost, the porters believed it, and so did the regular signalmen, although nobody would admit to having seen it. Like all good ghost stories, this ghost was reputed to appear only at night, and then, only on foggy winter nights. Perhaps closing time at the pub opposite had something to do with it, but all the station staff pointed out that they would not like to be the signalman on duty all alone on a deserted platform when the ghost was due to appear. The regular signalman kept the door locked, and nothing would induce him to go out on to the platform.

This story had continued for years, so when Ken and I came on the scene it was too good to be missed, we had to do something about it, if only to keep a good story going, so the ghost had to be resurrected. Ken started it off on the night turn. First he waited for the station to close down and to see the Station Master's bedroom light go out in the station house opposite, then he trundled a platform trolley from the Up platform over the crossing and on to the Down platform, keeping out of sight under the overhang of the roof canopy. Mr. Wright opened his bedroom window, and through the fog, he could just make out the barrow moving, without being able to see Ken, but there was no move on his part to go and investigate. The next morning the station was full of this incident, the ghost was about again, but stories feed on stories, and now that we had brought the ghost back to life, it was time to build on it, so I took a hand in enlarging the rumours.

I had to wait a couple of weeks until it was my turn to be on the night shift, and to have a foggy night, because there was no point in rushing things, after all, if a job's worth doing, it's worth doing well. During the afternoon, Ken set the stage, bringing the ghost into every conversation, priming the station staff so that their thoughts were orientated ghost-wise, so by the time that I came on at ten, they were jumping at their own shadows in the station lights.

At 11.30 p.m., after the last train had gone, the late turn porter shut off the station lights, and came up into the signal box with the keys. He did not notice the end window open, or the ball of cotton waste, which I had scrounged off the Abingdon branch engine driver, soaking in a bucket of water, he just left the keys and with a parting remark about locking the door to keep out the ghost, he made his way back up the platform towards the gate. I could hear his steel-heeled boots on the flagstones, regular steps, brave steps, he was not afraid of any old ghost, then I threw that ball of cotton waste, heavy with water. I could not see its flight, but I did hear it drop with a flop just behind him, and the result was most encouraging. There was a half-strangled shriek, then the gate slammed, and hob-nailed boots went like the clappers up the road, over the bridge, and down into the village. As I retrieved the cotton waste, not wishing to leave any evidence around and spoil things, I could see that water had splashed everywhere, and so another aspect was added to the story, the ghost came from the river. That porter is no longer a railwayman, but he still lives in the village, and he still recalls the night when the ghost nearly had him. I sit in the corner of the pub sometimes, and listen to this, and wish that I could put the clock back twenty-five years, I could really put on a show now, with a tape recorder and some organ music.

As the winter closed in, the couple of days I had owing to me for working on bank holidays came in useful, as my new house was ready at Kennington, so I had the time off and moved from Didcot, borrowing a railway lorry and container for the furniture, and returning to Didcot for my family. We were tipped out on to the platform at Radley on a dirty night, with fog, drizzle and a long way to go on the bus, and there was my wife with the two children, I had a budgie in a cage, a goldfish in a bowl, and a lively puppy on a lead, all of us cold and tired. I began to wonder what I had done to deserve this, just one week before Christmas, then the bus came along and we piled in. We settled down for the four-mile run, but half way along the road, the driver missed one of the twisting curves and put the near-side wheels into the ditch. We stepped out onto a muddy ploughed field and went home to find the fire had gone out. Only a railwayman used to roughing it could have got over that introduction to Kennington, but it would be worth it, in the long run, as I was now at the half way mark of my district.

The car factories at Cowley were now really beginning to attract away railway labour, so much so that it was impossible to continue with rest days, the labour was so short, and it was easier to pay the lads overtime for their day off, so rest day relief was broken up and our circuit with it, and we were all absorbed into regular relief work. That did not mean that I would lose Ken's company, as we were to overlap, almost as much as before, and it used to please me to see him come puffing up the steps of a signal box to relieve me, knowing that, after all these months, he still had not found out about the two bricks I had put in his saddle bag, or that I had tightened down his rear brake blocks. I had gained some satisfaction to make up for those cow kale plants.

My first job after moving house to Kennington, was to cover a vacancy at Sandford, and very nice it was too. I could see the box from my garden, so it was just a case of hopping over the fence and up the line for half a mile, with the added advantage of being paid lodging allowance for it. The agreement was, that any box under three miles distant, was paid walking time, based at the rate of twenty minutes to the mile, but any box outside that distance was a lodging turn, paid at the rate of 7/6d or 37½p for each turn, and the tricks we got up to so that we got home and still drew that lodging money, I will come to later, it was a tax-free bonus and we grasped it with both hands. It was swings and roundabouts in my case, with lodging pay for boxes near Kennington, but nothing for the Didcot boxes, because that was my home station. There were drawbacks at Sandford, including tilley lamps for lighting, no water and no toilet, which was ludicrous really, with the sewerage works right behind the box, and there was the dubious advantage of the filter beds, the aroma coming off them on a misty summer morning or during the evening at the end of a hot day, was very uplifting, and we were never bothered with flies or wasps, even they couldn't breathe it.

It was here, in the Sandford box, that I had the pleasure of training a new man: Chris Boyne came to fill the vacancy, and in much the same way as I had gone to Milton, but without the benefit of the Reading Signal School. Chris was brand new to railway work, so we had to begin from scratch, but he was a willing learner. I began very quietly with him, explaining over and over again, then setting studies for him to do at home. I had the advantage of a railway background, but what seemed simple to me, was hard for Chris. Week after week I hammered away at him, and then suddenly it all began to fall into place and make sense to him, and after that, there was no looking back. He told me long afterwards, that several times he had been on the point of packing it all in, but that I had been so patient with him, it would have not been fair to do so. Three months to the day, Bill Checkley came and gave him an examination, and Chris passed, and the next day he had to go up to Paddington where he passed again. When he took over I was as pleased as he was, and he never let me down, he ran that signal box as if he had been born into signalling.

I now moved into Kennington signal box, and came up against the village bobby, P.C. Tony Hore. I knew Tony slightly through seeing him in the village, he was a good copper, one of the old school, who believed in a clip round the ear instead of juvenile court, for any youngster misbehaving, but what I caught him at one afternoon, was right outside police behaviour, or so I thought at the time.

My first sighting of him, on this particular afternoon, was of him on the river bank poking away in the water with a long stick. He was there for an hour, then he climbed over the fence and came up into the box, which was not unusual, as a lot of the city police used to come to the box for a warm and a cup of tea, but this was afternoon, not night-time. He changed out of his wellington boots and into his shoes, as if it was an everyday affair that he had been up to, then he asked if he could use the telephone.

He rang Oxford city police, and very kindly informed them that they had a body in the water on their side of the river, then he hung up and turned to me, grinning all over his face. As he said, it saved him a lot of paper work, and they had done the same to him a few weeks before. Tony was a man after my own heart, I could appreciate the situation.

Some weeks later at Kennington, I saw Bill Checkley go into action and show just what a good railwayman he was, and it was the first time that I had a signal wire break. The weather was bad, the wind howling and the rain battering up against the window, and I had a 'Royal' booked up at 11.00p.m. from Oxford, so Bill Checkley (as was his habit when 'Royals' were about in his district) arranged to go to one of the signal boxes to see it go by, and this time, he decided to come to Kennington. He parked his little car in the lane tight up against the hedge and battled his way over the level crossing, content to sit in the chair near my roaring fire, until the train had passed. I received the 'call attention' one beat on the block bell, then after I had acknowledged it back to Hinksey South, the 'Royal' train code came through, 4–4–4 on the bell. I repeated the sequence to Sandford then went to the Up starting signal to pull off, and really swung into that lever as it was a heavy pull with the signal being so far away. As I lifted the clip and opened my shoulders, there was a loud bang downstairs, and I went crashing across the box to land up against the lockers on the other side, because the signal wire had broken.

The shocked look on Bill's face was something to see as I picked myself up. Bill shot out of the chair and even forgot his trilby hat, he went down the tall outside stairway sliding on his hands on the stair rails, grabbed my hand lamp and was off up the line on my bike, coat tails flying, and shouting over his shoulder 'repeater'. Then I understood, Bill was going to try to beat the train and hold up the counter balance weight of the signal so that it would be in the off position. The 'Royal' was blowing up for my distant signal when I saw the little signal show off in the glass case, I pulled off my home signal and heard a satisfactory toot on the engine whistle. The 'Royal' went thundering past under the window, the driver, fireman and inspector looking up at me with an enquiring look on their faces. Little did they know of our efforts to give them a clear road.

Bill returned to the box, wet through and wind-blown, his hands bruised and bleeding, but he had done a great job, and one that I admired him for. After he had gone, I had a rough couple of hours until the signal linesmen had repaired the wire, as I had to stop all Up trains and instruct the drivers to pass that signal showing a red light, all part and parcel of railway work which the public never knew about.

The next week brought extra work to Kennington as a result of a derailment at Harrow and Wealdstone. We had heard rumours, because news like that travels swiftly round signal boxes, even if it is in another district or another railway, but even we were not prepared for the magnitude of it until the details began to filter through. Being signalmen, we could feel the anguish that the signalman must be going through, to have seen that happen right outside his box. As a result of the disaster, the trains were re-routed over the Princes Risborough branch and down through Kennington Junction, and it was a week before it slackened off, but now that bit of line is all ripped up, and a way of life is gone.

My next change came with a move to Wolvercote Junction for a couple of months, and it brought a bit of fun that we all enjoyed.

The box was situated under the bank of the Oxford to Witney main road, the A40, with the junction to Banbury curving away in front and the line to Yarnton, Worcester and Fairford cutting away behind. Across the other side of the main line was the Oxford canal, with a most attractive lock-keeper's cottage sited near the tow path. Although we had water supplied from Oxford in cans, we did, at times, go down to this cottage and draw water from the well, for it was pure spring water, far sweeter than our official supply, but the lock-keeper had a problem, undesirable tenants, and they were to give us several weeks of entertainment before they were dealt with. Floating in the cut-off from the canal was a converted war time landing craft, made into a houseboat. It was a smart little job with a big bay window at one end, and we could, in fact, see right down inside from the signal box, but the problem was that this houseboat was occupied by two 'ladies of pleasure', and, with a pair of binoculars, it was possible to see a lot. Binoculars, you may say, what would clean-living young signalmen require with those? Well now, Wolvercote canal backwater was a haven for kingfishers, and they formed a constant display of beautiful colours diving into the still waters as they fished. If they happened to be near the houseboat, then we saw other types of colourful birds, but the use of binoculars was official, since the lock-keeper wanted these girls moved on, and so did the County Police, but because of some long-forgotten law dating back to Queen Anne's time, a houseboat was protected providing that there were no more than two customers on board at any one time.

An approach was made to the railway by the police which resulted in Bill Checkley issuing a pass for the police to use the signal box as an observation post, so we had the company of a police constable on the early and late shift, he was equipped with binoculars, so what was more natural than for us to assist him, in between trains? We would see the paying guests arrive in cars and they would park them on the grass verge up on the bridge, then they would creep down the tow path and into the boat. They must have known about that old law, because there was never more than two at a time on board, and yet in the evenings, the traffic was so heavy, that the two coming out used to pass the two going in. It went on for weeks, and the police were becoming concerned, as not only was it wearing out the path, it was causing severe eye-strain to the officers and ourselves from those high-powered glasses, so steps had to be taken that were outside the law.

I came on one afternoon in the middle of the week to relieve Ken and take up my observation duties, only to find the boat gone and also the policeman, but we both put on a brave face about it, and blinked back the tears, and then Ken told me what had happened. At ten in the morning, both girls had gone tripping up the path, as young girls do, arms round each others' waists, gaily chatting away, their shopping bags swinging. It was a beautiful morning, business was good, so a trip into Oxford would do no harm, and they waited on the road for a lift, and it was not long before some kind person took pity on two innocent young ladies and gave them a lift.

Ken said that it was then that the policeman in the box went into action, and was on the phone to Witney in a flash to report that the boat was empty. Within twenty minutes a police van drew up on the bridge and the police driver came running down the path and into the signal box, where he began to strip off and put on a pair of swimming trunks. He then opened a bag which he had brought with him and took out a whacking great carpenter's brace with a two inch bit. His next move was to swim over to the boat, take a quick look around and a deep breath, and then he was under the water, coming up now and again for another gulp of air.

It took half a dozen dives before he climbed out of the canal, and by the time he had returned to the box, the water was lapping at the bay window as the boat settled, then there was a lot of disturbance in the water, and the boat gently slipped under the surface of the canal, leaving the roof outlined a foot below.

When those girls returned, Ken said that even across the width of the canal, and across four running lines, and with the windows of the box closed, he could still hear the langauge of those girls! They went back up the tow path and we never saw them again, and in October a farm tractor dragged the houseboat out and took it away.

Signal box work was full of incidents which still stand out in my memory. Wolvercote Junction was the only place that I ever had the horror of horrors for a signalman, namely having two trains in the section at the same time, and, to make matters worse, on a foggy morning, and like all incidents of this nature, it happened so simply.

Wolvercote Sidings box was switched out so I was working with Bert Allen, another relief signalman at Oxford North Junction. Bert's signal box controlled the south exit from Oxford locomotive shed, and in the early mornings two movements were booked out. First a diesel railcar that went to Kingham, and then a light engine that went to Yarnton yard. On this particular morning, the diesel railcar came up to the shed signal, out of sight of Bert in the fog, but instead of letting Bert know that he was there, the driver sat in the cab and started to make up his ticket. The light engine came up behind him, and the fireman telephoned Bert that the engine was there and ready to leave, so Bert asked me for 'line clear' on the block bells, so I gave him the road, releasing the block so that he could pull off his signals, and away went both of them, down the main line towards me.

Bert could see what had happened as they went past, a few hundred yards separating them, but all he could do was to phone me, and keep his fingers crossed. There was only one course of action open to me, and that was to watch the track circuit on the diagram and hope that I wouldn't hear a bang under the road bridge. The track circuit lit up, and a moment later the diesel railcar swept by, then I slapped back the signals and changed the points over for the Banbury line, just as the circuit lit up again with the light engine.

It had been a nasty moment, but we got both drivers together and squared it up. Both Bert's register and mine showed nothing wrong, so we had got away with it, but Bill Checkley knew that something had happened, but he couldn't get to the bottom of it, as we had closed ranks all round, both locomotive and traffic departments; we had to, or we all would have been for the 'chop'.

One Sunday morning, years later, when Bert had retired and I had left the service, there was a single line working on the main line at the bottom of my garden, and Bill Checkley saw me in the garden and came over for a chat. We sat down in the kitchen and had a cup of tea, then the whole story came out, it was still bothering Bill after all those years, so I told him what had happened, and he went away happy, because he didn't like mysteries.

Kidlington box was our limit down the Banbury line, and it was like having a day off to be sent there. It was a big box with a large frame, tucked into the bank on the Up side about a hundred yards from the station, but the large frame was a left-over from more prosperous times, because nowadays, the booked service was light, with only the Blenheim and Woodstock branch running in and out to connect with stopping passenger trains.

The cross-over was a sight to see however. I knew from my footplate days that the road was always rough there, and now I could see the reason, because the rails had been laid across a bog. The ganger had packed tons of ballast under that cross-over, but within a few weeks the mud and water would seep up, and when an express came thundering over it, the whole lot would lift up between the wheels, showering a thick yellow mud everywhere. At times, as the engines lurched, it looked as if they would come crashing into the end of the signal box, and I used to get a bit concerned about it, but it didn't seem to bother the regular men who had got used to the situation, and I suppose it was safe enough.

Opposite the box was Campsfield, the Borstal correction school, and Kidlington airfield lay behind that, so there was always something going on to relieve the boredom. One day, as the Down stopper ran in, some of these Borstal boys arrived with their escorts to go to the school, and as I watched them get out, I saw one of them make a dash for it, running as hard as he could down the path towards me. There were people chasing him and shouting for somebody to stop him, and I thought I had better do something about it, so down the steps I ran, holding out my arms, which was all I could think of on the spur of the moment. The lad came on towards me, a hulking great kid with hands the size of footballs, and I began to wish that he was going in the opposite direction and that I was chasing him. However, I stood my ground, feeling that the honour of the Company was at stake, then he saw me and stopped, and with a look of complete despair on his face, he burst into tears. Poor kid, whatever he had done to be sent to Campsfield, it must have been bad, but I felt sorry for him, and hoped that he turned out all right in the end.

Chapter Five

Consolidation

When the holiday period was over and all the lads were back in their boxes, Bill Checkley recalled me and I became 'spare' for a few weeks. It had been a tiring period, for I had been on duty seven days a week for twenty seven weeks, without a break, but rather than sit about in the office, I asked if I could go out into the district and learn some of the other signal boxes. Bill agreed to this arrangement, because he knew where to find me if I was wanted, so I learned my way around Didcot North Junction, Moreton, Cholsey and Didcot West End boxes, then later I had a day at Aston Tirrold, and a few days down the Fairford branch. In that way I was doing myself a favour, financially speaking, because the more boxes that I signed for, the less spare work I would do, 'spare' meant just the bare hours with no allowance for walking or overtime, and with two children in the family I needed every penny that I could lay my hands on. It was while I was learning Carterton box, that I got landed with the branch for a couple of weeks; Bill rang me up and asked me to cover the late turn duty the next day, and I agreed. The box was right opposite the big American air base, in fact, some of the big bombers were parked on dispersal pads behind the box, having to cross the single line to return to the base.

It was full of take-offs and landings all day, a succession of big swept-wing bombers roaring over the top of the box, and they were so low that I could see the rivets in the panels, and as I was most interested in these big aircraft, the next day I brought a high-powered ex-naval telescope with me, through which I spent a happy hour watching close up, the air activity. Suddenly, the box door burst open, and I was confronted by two very large American Air Force Police. They both held six-shooters and pointed them directly at me, it was like looking down the front of a cannon.

These colonials meant business, and explanations took time. Even when I pointed out that my family went back to 1066, long before the *Mayflower*, they still took away my telescope, and I believe they would have taken me too, if it had not been that a ground crew wanted to move a parked bomber across the line, and I was the only one there able to take care of the railway side of the operation. I had to ring Bill Checkley and tell him what had happened, because, apparently, a letter was on the way to him from the White House, containing objections to my close scrutiny of the U.S. aircraft. Bill sniffed, and made remarks like 'What about going to Fairford for a week to keep out of mischief', so that is what I had to do, but the story has a happy ending, in that I got my telescope back a month later.

I worked the late turn at Fairford without having learned the box in advance, but it was fairly simple, even if I had to do the jobs of the signalman, ticket collector and porter at times. There was a weighbridge at Fairford which was right outside my powers of comprehension, so I used to trust the farmers and the coal merchants to weigh the loads and just give me the tickets. When the last train from Oxford had run in, the little tank engine went to shed, leaving me all on my own, and it was my job to lock up the station and turn out the lights, but not before checking the toilets, to make sure that they were empty. It was the first time that I had been in the ladies' toilets, and I was most surprised to find that the writings on the walls were far more interesting than those in the gents, quite educational in fact, and it took me a week to read them all.

Once the station was secured, I had to put the keys through the letter-box of the early turn signalman's house, which was only just across the station yard, then I would mount my bike and cycle all the way to Swindon, catching the 1.40a.m. parcels for Oxford, the driver very kindly stopping at the bottom of my garden to let me get off. Doing it that way, and catching the train from Oxford for the next duty, meant quite a long round trip, but it saved the lodging turn money, which was worth a couple of pounds a week, and I would far rather have the money for my wife, than hand it over to a landlady.

When Bill thought he had punished me sufficiently over the Carterton incident, he called me in and sent me to Milton for a week. Again, now that I was living at Kennington it meant a long cycle ride each day, but on this occasion it was worth it.

Once every twenty years or so, depending on the state of the passenger receipts, goods returns, wage increases and such-like, the company would discover, much to their surprise, that they had too much money, so there would be enough to allow for redecoration of signal boxes. When repainting was planned, signalmen hoped to be on holiday or off sick for a couple of weeks, because trying to run a busy signal box with three or four painters around was nearly impossible.

The first indication as to what was in store would come when a signalman was placing his cycle inside the frame room, and would see two dozen one-gallon tins of chocolate and cream paint in the corner, together with half-gallon tins of red, blue, yellow and black for the levers. There was enough paint to cover Paddington station, but the painter knew from bitter experience, that once a tin of cream or chocolate had been opened, unless it was used up that day, it would evaporate mysteriously during the night, but it was only Newton's Third Law of Notion, at work, for every action there is an equal reaction, and it was their cunning against our empty coffee jars. There was no excuse for any signalman to own a rusty bike, and I decided that locking-bar blue was just the colour for mine, chocolate and cream fitted nicely into the colour scheme of the bathroom and toilet at home, while signal lever red came in handy for the window-sill tiles. The white was useful for the window frames, but I never did find a use for the yellow, so that particular can remained full.

These painters would travel down from Reading each day, big portly men, taking an hour to walk from the station, and when they arrived it would be time for a cup of tea, so they would be with us a long time. Once the battle began it would start with the removal of dust, all the windows would be opened and the brushing-off started, dust that was laid an inch thick on the cross-beams. After two days, when this had either blown out of the window, or settled back down on the rafters, beams, roof and walls, as far as half-way down would change from blackened puce to cream, and the lower half together with lockers, table, chairs and even the broom handle, would become chocolate, all giving off a heavy stinging aroma of good old-fashioned lead paint. Our meat and cheese sandwiches would taste of paint, and we washed them down with a cup of paint-flavoured tea. The next procedure was for the painters to go away for a couple of weeks, and then return to paint the window frames, if there was any white paint left! Once that was done, it would be the turn of the levers, and it was not long before our hands, lever cloths and trousers were covered in red, black, yellow and white paint. Finally they would be gone, leaving us with another twenty years to scrape paint off the window-glass and paint spots from our, once, highly polished, floor. They were not a bad lot of lads, they never reported the loss of paint, and they had a job to do, so it was quite unfortunate for them that they were the only people not welcome in a signal box.

I found that Sunday engineering working made a nice change and an interesting time acting as hand signalman clipping points under the direction of the signalman in the box, or acting as Pilotman during single line working, when one line was occupied by the engineers. It was very interesting to see miles of relaying in progress, with signal gantrys and cross-overs being ripped out to be replaced by new, and if there was a big job in another district, we would be sent there to assist. Reading and London were the most usual places for us to be sent, and I always looked forward to working with the Cockney boys. They were a good lot of lads, and took good care of us, particularly where the underground electric lines ran, because, in the dark, it was easy to step on to the live rail, as we were not used to it. When they came to our district, we would look after them too, because they were not used to fast-running trains, as everything in their district was either just starting out of Paddington or slowing down to run in, but they did not like tilley lamps.

I was sent up to Old Oak Common East Box one Saturday evening with Gerald Massey, one of the Oxford relief men, both of us expecting to spend our time clipping points, as the job we were involved in was a big relaying operation that spanned the whole of the weekend. When we walked up into the box to report to Bill Odey, the District Inspector, he confronted us with 150 tilley lamps which had been laying dormant for years. In the London district, if a signalman wanted a light, he pulled down a switch and a light appeared, but a tilley lamp was filled with paraffin, it had a gas light mantle, and you had to pump it up. The London chaps had tried one, but once it started to spit and pop, spraying paraffin all over the place, they threw it into a bucket of water and sent out an appeal to Bill Checkley, so we country boys were sent up to cope with the lamps. Bill Odey was more than pleased to see us, as he badly needed those lamps outside, so Gerald and I set to work cleaning, filling and priming those lamps all night, and the next night too, so in fact, we never got outside to see what was going on.

I seized every available chance to travel on the footplate, so I caught the train at Didcot, joining Gerald who had got on at Oxford. He thought I was 'eleven pence short of a bob' because I obtained permission to have a go on the shovel, and when the firemen saw that I could handle locomotive work, they would sit down to enjoy a break, in fact, one fireman soon got into the coach when we stopped at Reading, and left the firing to me.

I had four footplate trips that weekend, two Up and Down, and on the last trip home on the Sunday morning, it was with a 'County', one that I had not had a go at before. We had walked up to Paddington to catch this parcels train, so I stopped when we reached the engine cab and asked the driver if I could come up on the footplate, and have a look, as I had never been on the footplate of a 'County' class locomotive. He was most pleased to let me have a look, and when I told him that, until four years previous, I had been a fireman for years, the invitation that I was angling for was offered, and, for the first time ever, I had a chance to fire a 'County'.

This 'County' was the first one built, No. 1000 *County of Middlesex* and it was a surprise to me to find that the cab and boiler front were as big as those on a 'King' and when I looked inside the firebox, I found that it was the same size as a Churchward 47XX, it seemed to go on for ever. Had I lost touch with a big firebox, I wondered? Looking along that fat squat boiler to see the double chimney sitting on top of the smoke box, gave me the feeling that this was a locomotive with power to spare, it ought to have plenty with the steam pressure needle hovering on 280lb, I had never worked with such high pressure before.

The fireman gave me a few tips, such as keep the back corners tight and well up under the flap, and build her up to a thick wedge of fire that fills the box from side to side, leaving a gap under the brick arch, so that the coal can reach the front; he might just as well have told me to pack as much into her as she would hold! The driver, Tom Evans, opened up the ejector and blew off the brakes, the ejector sounding harsh as the jet of steam roared up through the chimney. He placed her in full fore gear and we started off, those big cylinders taking the steam, then sending it back to exhaust out of the chimney, not with the crisp, short bark of a 'Castle' marching out, but with a sound very new to me, exhausting with a brutal beat, each one cut off cleanly, each one to slam up against the underside of Westbourne Terrace bridge as we pulled away.

I pulled up the flap as Tom shut off to let her roll over the newly relaid section, looking down at the lads collecting up the tilley lamps, answering back the ribald comments thrown up at me, then, once clear I saw the big counterbalance weight come down as Tom lifted the regulator half way over, and the power began to show, slamming the flap up against the firehole. The fireman standing up in the corner looked over at the pressure gauge, and began to look a little apprehensive, as if wanting to say something, but not liking to interfere, so I took the hint and picked up the shovel and began to fire her. She took the coal from the shovel almost before I could get it in, then Tom wound back the lever so that I could dig the shovel down into the back corners and under the doors. I began to fill her up, the memory of my firing methods all coming back to me as I packed the coal in, first dribbling it under the doors, then straight down the middle, and the lovely bit of burnt Welsh coal mixed with the exhausting steam and drifted over the roof of the cab and onto the footplate.

Through Acton the exhaust injector went on, and I was firing her again through Ealing Broadway and West Ealing, and the red needle touched the 280lb mark and she began to sizzle from the safety valve. The fireman looked at me and grinned, seeing that I had her on the boil, and he relaxed and sat on the seat, reaching over to drop and lift the flap between each shovelful. Tom eased down over Hanwell viaduct, enough for the exhaust injector to blow out, and then she lifted her safety valve, roaring enough to waken the sleeping town, so on went the live steam injector to quieten her, only for a few minutes, just enough to return the glass full of bobbing water up out of sight, then we tore through Southall. Hayes and West Drayton slipped past, and I picked up the shovel again, firing her all the way through Iver and Langley. She was certainly living up to the reputation that I had heard about the 'Counties', scoffing coal as fast as I could feed her. I wouldn't have cared to fire her on the 'Cornishman', firing non-stop for four hours, and though I had heard that they were shy on steaming, this particular one wasn't, it was only the exhaust injector which was keeping her from blowing off, the needle was stuck fast on 280lb with just a whisp of steam coming out of her brass bonnet.

As we passed Taplow I could see the familiar piles of rusty barbed wire, still there years after the war was over, and it was obvious that they had not moved at all during the years that I had been away. We then tore over Maidenhead bridge, the sound echoing back from the sleeping town below, through Twyford and once past the big power station, Tom shut off steam and we free-wheeled into Reading for a ten minute booked stop. This gave us time for a chat, and Tom and his mate chivvied me for leaving footplate work and urged me to go back, but I told them that was impossible, as I had lost my seniority, and I was well contented with a relief signalman's life, it was just that a little run like this kept my hand in. In real life one can never go back, only in books such as this.

I sat down on leaving Reading, because I was so tired after having been up since the afternoon of the day before, and having worked all night, but I did ask if I could use the scoop over the water troughs at Goring. It had been so many years since I had used one, but the water came flooding in as if it was yesterday, the float rising up until the water began to gurgle in the vents, and we were full again.

We drifted around the Didcot avoiding loop towards Didcot North Junction, and I sat on the seat peering out over my old engine shed, to see the familiar locomotives that I had known for years, row upon row of them, the smoke drifting out of their chimneys as they waited for another day's work. We clattered over the points and swept down towards Appleford, the signalman with his hand on the Down distant signal lever ready to return it into the frame, and I could see the look of surprise on his face, as he spotted me peering round the side of the cab. We then flashed past, over Nuneham bridge, through Culham, pounding on to Radley, the clang of the shovel ringing out over the sound of this lovely engine hard at work. We passed through Radley, and on approach to Sandford, Tom shut off and allowed the engine to drift. I shouted to Chris in the box, and as he slid back the window, I pointed forward with my hand, he nodded his head, understanding my charade of signs, so I shook hands with Tom and his mate and climbed down the foot steps, jumping clear onto the ballast easily from long practice. Tom gave a short blast on the whistle as I walked up my garden path, and I was grateful to him and his fireman, for they had given me one of the most enjoyable Sunday engineering turns of duty that I had ever had. It had been the first time on the footplate for a long long time, and I began to wonder if there would be another time, but if that was one of the best Sundays, the next weekend was to bring the worst, and one that I never want to see again, even if I did return to the footplate for a few brief moments.

That week I was 'spare' for a couple of days, then I went to Foxhall Junction to cover the early turn for the rest of the week. It was in November, dismal days with just enough fog to make working difficult, but not foggy enough to call out the fogmen. I had a busy time with trains out of the Didcot ordnance depot and engines coming from the Down relief into the depot yard and then finding margins to let them out, and the freight traffic from the West Curve came at awkward moments, they needed a long margin to cross the junction and over into the Down loop to Milton. In fact, if an express had left Swindon on the Up main, and another was through Reading on the Down main, there was no chance at all to move across the junction from the West Curve. Once I had cleared the curve, the transit traffic from Didcot yard via North Junction would be on the move, and it was an involved operation for both of us, to get this traffic into the depot.

My problem was with the War Department Police. I had to get on the phone to them, usually at breakfast time, and prise one of them out of the mess room to walk down to the depot gate and unlock and open it, and that chap knew that he could expect to be there standing about in the cold for perhaps an hour. This was because now the gate was open, I could let the signalman at North Junction know, and he, in turn, had to allow the transfer trip with 70-odd wagons propelled by a 57XX pannier tank to go from the yard across his junction and into the Appleford Down loop. After this he was able to change his points, obtain 'line clear' from me and give the little engine the chance to charge off. It had to be a full-blooded charge with the driver confident that the gate was open, because he couldn't see it from the other side of Foxhall bridge, and once committed with those wagons on the move, it was a fight between the weight of the train and the tight curve binding the wheels.

In the box we could hear the struggle, but we could not see what was going on because of the trees and earth works, so we had to rely on the depot policemen ringing up and informing us that the train was inside the depot, complete with tail lamp, thus enabling 'train out of section' to be given to North Junction and another train accepted.

Depot policemen could not seem to understand the importance of that little oil lamp, and they would close the gate and just clear off, leaving me stranded with 'train on line' on the block, and North Junction tied up too. We had repeatedly tried to explain the situation, and in the past we had phoned, written reports and asked Bill Checkley to look into it, and things would improve for a couple of days, then it would be back into the old routine. I decided to take things into my own hands, and rang the Commanding Officer, and, by sheer luck, I got through to him instead of some orderly clerk. I asked this gentleman if he could spare the time to come into the box the following morning, to see the problem, and he agreed.

It was sheer luck how it worked out on the following day, as this officer came into the box just before the depot trip was due and he turned out to be a Royal Engineer who had been on the Longmore Military Railway. When the trip came round the curve, the policeman cleared off, as usual, but we had a troop special booked for ten minutes later, and there I was with the block tied up back to North Junction. The officer was as good as his word, he was out of the box and into the depot in no time, and whatever he did must have worked, for I had no further trouble from the depot policemen. However, I received a mild rocket from Bill Checkley for by-passing him, and a request for me to work at Foxhall as groundsman for engineering work on the Sunday.

I accepted the extra overtime, as it seemed a simple job to do and I didn't have to start until 7.00a.m; the engineers' occupation was near the Up main Home signal, and all trains, including passenger trains, would have to travel over the Up goods loop from Milton, so all that I had to do, was put a clip on the facing points and hold a green flag up. Considering the light Sunday traffic I should be home again by three in the afternoon.

The mist cleared as the 'Red Dragon' came sweeping up the main line, the gentle curve stretching back to Milton giving me a panoramic view of this greyhound streaking towards me, the smoke rolling back along the roofs of the coaches. As 'Britannia' No. 70026 *Polar Star* roared through the jumble of rods connected to the driving wheels seemed so mixed-up when compared to the sleekness of a 'Castle'. She bucked a little as she rode over my junction, tucking the mixture of smoke and steam in behind the last coach and making me look hard for the tail lamp. She was a familiar sight on this train, now that the 'Castles' had been moved on, sharing the run on the 'Red Dragon' with *Ariel*. Little did I know then, that when I saw her the following day, she would be in a very different position.

That next morning, Sunday, 20th November 1955, according to my diary, I went on duty and found Jack Drew in the box. I carried a point clip down to where I should need it, together with a red and green flag, then I went up the path and over the bridge to Jackson's for the Sunday papers. As I left the little shop, the mist began to clear, and by the time the engineering train took up position on the Up main line, there was the promise of the sun coming through. We had a leisurely morning, I had only eleven trains to deal with, so I helped Jack to clean and polish, being glad of something to occupy my time between trains. At midday we stopped and had a pot of tea and some sandwiches, as there was nothing due up until the Treherbert excursion just after one in the afternoon. I was able to renew my contact, by telephone, with Granville Burt, as he was down the line at Milton box, and I had not seen him for some time. Whilst we were speaking, his block bell rang calling his attention to the Up excursion, so I rang off, knowing that it would soon be time for me to go down to the loop points and deal with this train, which was approaching the speed restriction.

Granville asked for 'line clear' from Foxhall and as the block bells rang, I made to move down the stairs. As I reached the top the loop and Down main bells began to ring out, an urgent rapid beat as they were intended to, 'Emergency, call attention'. Jack acknowledged the call with one beat on the bell key, then from Milton came the worst bell signal of all, slow and distinct, so that there could be no mistaking it — 'ting, ting, ting, ting, ting, ting' meaning, 'Obstruction, danger'.

Jack and I looked at each other, wondering what on earth had happened, then the telephone rang and Jack answered it. He listened for a moment then turned towards me, his face ashen with shock. He had just been told by Granville that the excursion had gone down the bank and into the fields. I tore down the steps, only stopping to snatch up my bike, and got to the loop points where I quickly took off the clip in case Jack needed those points later, and as I passed the engineering train on the Up main line, I shouted out what had happened, then I was off down the path towards Milton as fast as I could pedal. As I got nearer to Milton box, I could see that something was badly wrong. There were a couple of coaches standing on the main line, and several more skewed over at an angle, but no-one could have been prepared for the sight that met my eyes when I got to the signal box. The 'Britannia' *Polar Star* was down the bottom of the bank on her side, and I remember thinking that her 6 feet 2 inches driving wheels looked so thin, she looked almost like a 'Hornby' engine that had jumped the rails, and there were coaches piled on top of her.

I went straight up into Milton box to see if Granville was all right. He wouldn't let me relieve him, and said that if he walked out then he could never return to a signal box again. Later, when it was all over, he described to me the dreadful shock of seeing that engine tearing towards him, disregarding the speed limit and then seeing it come lurching through the points from the main line into the loop, bucking and leaving the rails before plunging down the bank, taking the coaches with it.

When I left Granville he told me that the fireman had gone back towards Steventon with detonators to protect the derailment, so I could now concentrate on rescue work. The scene was appalling. Out of the ten coaches, five were off the rails and the leading four coaches had followed *Polar Star* down the bank and were badly damaged. I crawled into the cab of the engine to see if the driver was still in there, but it was empty, apart from coal scattered in a heap all over the cab side. One of the coaches was perched up over the side of the tender and cab, and another was telescoped up behind it, the underframe and wheels which had been sheared off were lying across the loop and the Up main line.

As I crawled out of the cab, the Ordnance Depot Fire Brigade and police began crowding over the fence with ladders, propping them up against the sides of the coaches and pulling the dead and injured up through the doors and shattered windows. I heard a cry for help, and immediately crawled under the underframe of the coach that had sheared off, to find a young man, pinned down by the coach frame lying across his middle. There was nothing I could do for him except to hold his hand and talk to him, and share several of my cigarettes with him. With the arrival of the rescue train, Dr. Horan from Didcot crawled in and alongside us both and gave the poor chap a shot in the arm to ease his pain, then he left to attend to others. I stayed with the young man until the jacks were placed under the frame, but just as the pressure was eased, the poor chap died holding my hand.

The next few hours were the worst hours of my railway career. I worked non-stop, helping to recover the dead and injured people, until two o'clock the next morning, when Bill Checkley found me, my uniform torn and filthy and covered in blood. He made me go home, and I did so, but reluctantly, and only on the understanding that I could come back as soon as I felt that I had rested enough. As I left the scene, I could hardly believe that this was my beloved Milton, ablaze with portable electric lights flooding all over this great piled-up heap of tangled wreckage, with Swindon and Old Oak Common steam cranes lifting and slewing as they sorted out the priority lifts to enable trapped people to be reached. My poor wife was beside herself with worry when I finally reached home at half past two in the morning, as she had heard nothing of the disaster.

At ten the next morning, I was back at Milton again after a fitful sleep. The passengers who had survived injury were gone, together with those coaches which had been derailed; all that remained were the wrecked coaches, and they had been lifted clear so that the Up main line could be used again, although at reduced speed. I was very sorry to hear that Bill Checkley had been taken to hospital, as he had stumbled down the bank during the night and broken his ankle, so Freddie Blackhall was in charge, and I spent the day assisting him in every way that I could. *Polar Star* was still in the field on her side, and she was to remain there for two weeks, sinking further into the mud as the water in her tank drained out, long after the other debris of the accident had been removed.

Long discussions took place as to how to get her back up the bank, for a 'Britannia' Pacific weighing 146½ tons with the tender, takes some moving, but the simple way in which it was achieved was something that I was lucky enough to see, and it was an education to watch when the operation eventually took place on Sunday, 4th December 1955.

During the previous week the relaying gang had been busy, all the damage to the track had been repaired and the signal department had renewed points, rodding and signal wires, so the box was fully operational again. Now it was the turn of the locomotive, and this was where the convenience of Milton depot came in. The gang built a track across the field from the sidings, even building a small bridge, from sleepers, over a ditch. Rails were then bolted to the wheels of *Polar Star* and she was lifted up by a steam crane into the upright position, then the rails attached to the wheels were connected up to the temporary track, the bolts were removed and she was carefully dragged out and into Milton depot, by a little pannier tank, then back up through Didcot depot where an engine was waiting to take her to Swindon for examination.

She had sustained some damage, of course, but not as much as I would have thought, because the ground had been soft and she had not hit another vehicle. A rail had gone up through the left-hand leading bogie and the frame, and then up behind the cylinder. The regulator rod was broken and she had lost her smoke deflector plate on that side, while a buffer from one of the coaches had punched a hole in the tender and allowed the water to drain out. The boiler cladding was crushed and covered in mud, but all in all, she got away with it fairly lightly, and within a few months she was again pounding up the main line to Paddington.

This railway accident had been the first one that had involved me in death and injury on a large scale; as I had cycled rapidly down the path that Sunday afternoon towards the scene, I had steeled myself to expect the worst, and I had indeed seen horrors that I hope I never see again. I was so busy once I got there that having to handle shattered bodies had no effect on me at the time. Only my wife knew what I had really gone through, as she would be woken by my restlessness in the early hours of the morning, and perhaps my colleagues thought me hard at the time, but as a result of this outward bearing, I was to be landed in another unpleasant task later, that of searching the line.

I had helped to carry this out many times when on the footplate, but other people had always been on the ground, we were just a means of conveyance. A light engine would go through the section with a recovery team, after any report of a door open on a passenger train. It was all part and parcel of working on the railway, a signalman would see that a door was open, so he would send to the box ahead the bell signal 'Stop and examine train' and telephone the reason, so the line had to be searched between that box and the one behind. Nine times out of ten it was a faulty door lock, but chances couldn't be taken, so a search was made, and I now became one of those on the ground, all because Bill Checkley thought that I was tough enough to go on such a job with him. Thank goodness I could only be called upon when I was 'spare' and available.

Once Bill and I searched the line between Didcot East Junction and Moreton on foot, Bill still limping from his injury at Milton. It was a dirty, wet evening as black as a coal mine, and we set off with only the flickering light of a hand lamp each to light our way, wondering what awful things we were going to find. All we knew was that the driver of a Down fast train had stopped and said that he thought he had seen someone fall off Moreton bridge. The first indication that anything, had, indeed gone wrong, was a shoe, with the foot still in it, and there were other bits and pieces of a body scattered over a hundred yards of track, but a 'King' with thirteen coaches behind doesn't leave much. The next step was for one of us to stop with the remains while the other went to the signal box and made arrangements for removal. To my discredit, I made sure that it was Bill who stopped there, I was off! Looking back on it now, the things that we had to do for nine and a half quid a week were far beyond the normal call of duty, but we accepted it then.

Cattle on the line could prove a real nuisance, holding up trains for some time. The first reports would come in from train crews, pulling up at the signal box to inform the signalman that there were either horses or cows on the line, so I would pass this information back to the signal box behind me, and the work would begin until the porters or relaying gang had cleared the section. My mate would stop all Up trains, and I would stop all Down trains, both of us acquainting the driver with the circumstances, and they were then allowed to proceed at reduced speed.

It was rough luck on expresses, which would urgently blow up on the whistle for the distant signal, reducing speed until they were nearly stopped, then the Home signal would be lowered to allow them to draw forward, only to be brought to a dead stop by a red flag from the box, so that information could be passed on. It knocked the stuffing right out of a run, but they were all good railwaymen and they understood, and it only happened now and again. Cows were not too bad, they could be rounded up fairly easily and returned to the fields, the gang then repairing the fence behind them, but horses were another matter, they would often gallop off down the line into another section so that two or more signalmen had to go all through the procedure of stopping trains until the horses were captured.

Once at Milton I saw a pack of hounds crossing the line while the huntsmen on their horses were milling about on the other side of the fence, shouting to those stupid hounds and helpless to avert what seemed a hopeless situation. The Up afternoon Pembroke train came tearing through under the bridge, the driver hanging on the whistle as he rocketed along in the eighties, but those hounds just ran round in circles completely confused. Then the driver acted in a way I wouldn't have thought of, he opened up the regulator and the cylinder steam cocks, and on a 'Britannia' it sounded as if the end of the world had come. Those hounds thought so anyway, and they took off, some of them clearing the fence with one leap to vanish into Milton depot, and when the train passed me, the driver was leaning out of the cab with his fireman, laughing at the sight of it all, but at least the hounds had got out of the way!

One hound became a pet in the home of one of the platelayers, simply because he refused to go home. When taken out for walks he would set off towards Steventon village away from the railway, and if trains were running on his return, he had to be dragged and carried back home.

Once at Culham, I had the report of a lion in the section between Radley and myself, so the usual procedure of warning trains was carried out, and it went on for some time because nobody from either Culham or Radley dared to walk through the section to find out. Then eventually, through the bridge towards me came nothing more exciting than a Great Dane, plodding his way up the main line. The poor old chap was confused and exhausted, and I caught him without any trouble and brought him up into the box where he drank a bucketful of water, then settled down until the police van collected him. They told me later that he had a cell to himself until his owner collected him, and he left behind two gallons of water over the floor!

No record about signal box work would be complete without a few pages devoted to a very important man rarely seen by the public, and that was the signal lamp man. The lad in our district was a diminutive Pole called Stefan, and one of the most cheerful little chaps imaginable, although he had one of the roughest jobs on the railway. In all weathers he would start going round the district each week beginning at Milton; we would all know that he was about, because the copper coil in the signal lamps would contract when he took the lamp out, and this would cause the contacts of the low voltage sensors to touch and ring the 'lamp out' bell in the signal box.

He would trim and fill his lamps in the small tin lamp hut near the box and then trudge off, his lamp stick loaded down with a dozen lamps suspended from it, all filled with long-burning oil. He would climb up tall Distant signal posts whilst a gale was blowing, hanging on for dear life if the signal was dropped. Sometimes, on a wet day, he would be wet through to his underclothes, and yet, I never heard him grumble.

Milton and Foxhall would take a day between them, whilst the big junction at Didcot East would take him all day, because, apart from the signals, he had all the ground signals to do, but he would beaver away, and by the end of the week he would be through to Sandford, ready to start the round again on Monday morning.

Now and again he would get a little overtime, a Sunday duty when signal box supplies were renewed, and on these occasions, a pannier tank with two coal wagons and a brake van would set off round the district, calling at each signal box with a drum of oil for Stefan, which he would unload, and ten hundredweight of coal for the signal box which a loco shed labourer would shovel out. This was supposed to be our supply for six months, but in a twenty-four hour box it lasted only about six weeks, that was why we were always scrounging coal from loco crews. Then on Monday morning Stefan would be back singing one of his Polish songs, happy now, that he had a new supply of oil and a Sunday duty paid at time-and-three-quarters.

I used to insist that he had his meal-break with me in the box, so that he could get warmed through on a cold day, and I also liked to know that he had a hot drink inside him before he went out again. In this way, I got to know him well, and I began to find out why he was so happy. Apparently it was because a few short years before he had been hungry and cold, working as a slave on fortifications in France after he had been shuttled back and forth between Germany and France, so although I thought he had a rough job, Stefan knew what a *really* rough job was, and he was so happy to have survived.

After all the overtime I had done, I had saved enough money to get mobile again, so I bought an old ex-army Norton side-valve motorcycle. It was a 500cc job and a great brute of a thing, as they say, it would 'climb the side of a house', and I got it at just the right time. The porter came from Radley one morning and called me out of bed, to tell me that Bill Checkley was in a spot, because the day shift man at Moreton Cutting box had reported sick at short notice, so the night man was still there and I was to go to Moreton as soon as I could, so off I set towards a signal box that I had never worked, and had learned two years before. On thinking about it though, perhaps that was the best way, to get pitched into a busy box before I could think about it. I relieved Eric Membery and he was gone in a flash leaving me with a full block, and it was a busy one with Up and Down main lines and reliefs carrying all of the traffic (that traffic I was used to at Foxhall), plus all the Oxford trains. Then I had an Up goods loop to contend with, and behind the box, the big marshalling yard with two pannier tanks blasting away all day, but I was in good company, I knew all the drivers and firemen, the engines were the same ones which I had fired in this very yard, and I knew the yard Inspectors and the shunters. One of them was, in fact, my brother-in-law, and I never had to fill a coal bucket or make a cup of tea, they looked after me so well. It was as well that they did look after me, because I wouldn't have had time to do it myself. I thanked my lucky stars that I had kept my little book with the lever movements written down in it, because I would never have had the time to work my way through the frame. My first move out of the yard, was to dispatch a light engine back to Didcot shed which meant turning him out of the yard on to the Up relief line, through the cross-over and down the relief. When I asked for 'line clear' from Didcot East, they gave it to me on the Down main, so I had another sequence of lever movements to go through, 26 to 30 levers, and at the same time I had to deal with other trains. It was no wonder that it took me several hours to 'play my way in'.

From the lofty height of the box, it was possible to see all over Moreton yard and to appreciate the work of the little pannier tanks. On four of the yard roads, the stop blocks at the far end of the sidings were mobile, each being a solid concrete block the size of a bungalow, riding on skids on the rails. These blocks would be pulled up the siding by the engine and then left with enough room for a couple of freight trains to be built up against them, then perhaps the last wagon going into that siding would be foul of the next line, so the pannier tank would be called in to squeeze them up. It was a sight worth watching. The little pannier would come gently in to buffer up, then with the sand trickling down on the rails and the safety valve blowing, it would push up all the loose wagon buffers until they were all compressed up against the concrete block, then the little engine would go down hard on her springs, her valves would groan in protest and, inch by inch, a thousand tons would begin to move, slowly, like some great ocean liner easing away from the dock side. Today, such a feat would be covered by television and a vast crowd, and yet, we took the power of the steam locomotive to be an everyday affair, and never gave it another thought.

I had two good weeks at Moreton, and it was to be the only time that I worked there, because the box is now gone along with the yard, but it had showed me that signal box work was as demanding as a hard-worked steam engine.

District Inspector'sOffice   Signalman H.Gasson,

Didcot   B.R.   Milton.

S.90419   1/2/52   3560

List No.45 Vacancy No.1769,Cl.1.District
Relief Signalman,Didcot.(Rest Day Relief)

In connection with the above,I have to inform you
Mr H.H.Briant has approved your appointment to this post.

Kindly note.

Chapter Six

End of an Era

The saddest time that I had as a relief signalman was when I had to see a signal box pulled down. The box was at Aston Tirrold, a signal box which I had learnt but never been called upon to operate. The box was an intermediate one between Moreton and Cholsey, with only twelve levers in the frame, a Home and Distant signal for each of the running lines and a detonator lever for each. The signalman there was a much-envied man, because the box was a day duty only, being closed between five in the evening and eight the next morning, but as with steam itself, the writing was on the wall, and the signal box was to be demolished, because automatic signals had been installed.

A month after the new automatic signals had been installed, I was given the duty to act as groundsman at Aston Tirrold, protecting the Up and Down relief lines, because the Signal and Telegraph Department had an occupation on the Up and Down main lines so that they could use a steam crane to demolish the signal box and remove the signals. I arrived at Aston Tirrold just in time to meet the train, which was pulled by a Collett 22XX class, taking up the occupation, which consisted of half a dozen low loaders and the steam crane with guard's van. My job was to make sure that when the steam crane began operating and the cab or jib was fouling the Down relief line, it was safe to do so, and I had to station myself well back towards Cholsey so that engine drivers could see me with my red and green flags.

The engine pushed the train back about fifty yards, then the van was uncoupled and left, and the wagons and crane drew forward to the signal box, and the gang began work. One section began disconnecting signal wires and rodding, while the other gang began knocking out bolts in the wall sections and roof. With a soft 'chuff, chuff' the crane began to work. The jib came round and the hook was connected to slings on the roof, and off it came in one section scattering roof tiles all over the place. As soon as the roof was laid on a low-loader, the front section was lifted out leaving the frame naked and bare, and within minutes that too was removed, leaving a gaping hole in the floor. The highly polished stove was ripped out without ceremony and thrown down into the waiting truck, to be followed by the table, chair and lockers, all so much junk now. The train was then pulled forward so that an empty truck stood under the shell, and the crane set to work again lifting out the remaining walls and steps; the coal bunker and lamp hut soon followed and then the site was laid bare, all that was left was a lot of churned-up ground covered with bolts, tiles, glass and wood fragments. Aston Tirrold signal box was no more, and another little bit of the Great Western had been laid to rest.

It was almost indecent to see the way in which the signal posts were removed; a chain was slung round the base, the little piston driving the flywheel flashed up and down and the jib began to rise with the pulley spinning round as the cable was wound back on the drum. The chain tightened, scrunching into the post and it began to quiver, then with a loud sucking noise, the post came out of the ground like a giant tooth, leaving a deep hole half full of muddy water. By three in the afternoon it was all over, the train had been coupled up and trundled down into Moreton yard, it had run round and transferred the brake van, then set off home to Reading, passing the empty site without so much as a glance.

The next day I was 'spare' and knowing that I would be called upon to cover Cholsey at the end of the week, I had a day there to refresh, which seemed necessary because it had been a year since I had learnt the box, and it was one job to which I did not look forward.

Cholsey signal box was part of the station. It sat squarely on the platform between the Up main line and the Down relief line. It had control of the Wallingford branch, but this was no problem as the 'Bunk', as it was known, operated just the same as the Abingdon branch, that is to say, one engine in steam, so that once the single line staff was handed over to the driver, it ran like a bus service, connecting with all the stopping passenger trains calling at Cholsey. The automatic signals had been installed on the east of Cholsey for a long time, replacing the box at South Stoke, so those at Aston Tirrold, on the west side, were an extension. The automatic signalling certainly speeded up train handling, but at the expense of the Cholsey signalman, for, in addition to his own work, he was now covering for those two removed signal boxes, working directly with Moreton and Goring on the block bells and instruments. The diagram was fully illuminated, and showed both the sections at each side, the automatic signals being released by levers in the box. These were full-size levers with the handle cut down but they still had to be pulled over to allow the electrical contact to be made, which in turn, showed up as a green light on the diagram where the intermediate signals were located.

Bill Palmer was on duty when I got there, and he was pleased to see me. The volume of traffic was such, that handling sixteen trains at once all travelling at express speeds with only a minute between was classed as normal working. Indeed, the custom of booking trains in the register was dispensed with, and only passing times were booked, so I was able to give him a break by taking over the Up traffic while he dealt with the Down, but from what I could see, I was in for a very busy time on Saturday.

I knew that day, when I left my old Norton motor-cycle in the station yard, that I would be mighty pleased to see it again after that duty. I took over with the block full, and as fast as I could get to one end of the frame to pull off, I had to be up at the other end putting signals back as the expresses roared through just a few yards away from me. Cholsey was the only signal box where I would have been glad to have been wearing roller-skates, because there came one period in the afternoon when the trains were running so tightly between each other, that I could not work fast enough and they began to receive Distant signal checks. Booking was out of the question, even the passing times; it was not the sort of place to come to, full up with tea, because a call of nature would have meant trains standing at signals, and there was no time for such mundane affairs. No one was more pleased than me to see his relief come, and I thanked my lucky stars that I did not work that box every day like the regular chaps. I will say this much for them, they were all thin lads, so obviously it was not the place for some of those portly signalmen.

On Monday, I went to Didcot North Junction to brush up on the box. I had not been there for a long time and it was a pleasure to work with Jack Gardener again, who had been one of the original 'mums' at Milton with the kitten. Jack was a signalman worth being with, he had been brought up in that world, being the fourth generation to go into the box. His grandfather was one of the original Didcot signalmen and Jack was very proud of the document that he showed to me, where his grandfather had been awarded £2.10.0d on July 3rd, 1891 for running his signal box without making any mistakes, a bit of Great Western history indeed. Whether or not he was a practical joker like his grandson, I don't know, but Jack was, as I found out to my cost. During my brush-up on the frame, I set the road out of the yard and into the Down goods loop ready for the transfer trip into Didcot depot.

Then I just had to go to the toilet, and with it came the chance that Jack was waiting for. The toilet was in a little smelly dirty hut with a tin roof, tucked under the outside stairway, and I had just entered when the wagons of the trip went rattling by just outside the door. Just then, Jack taped the lead straps of a fog detonator on the handle of the fire poker and dropped it out of the window, and down onto the tin roof. I remember at the time of the explosion thinking that we had another Appleford on our hands, because a few years previously, a goods train had run through the sand drag in the loop at Appleford, and the wagons following had smashed down the box, pitching the signalman, Gordon Churchman, into the field behind, together with the frame, but then, I could hear the wagons still rattling by, and the rust flakes from the roof began to subside, and I realised that I was safe, but it was half an hour before I dared come out.

I settled my nerves by having a cup of tea and sat down to read the special notices, after loosening the saddle-bolt on Jack's bike, by way of retaliation. These special notices were always interesting, about things like out of gauge loads, and ships' boilers and transformers, they all needed special attention, but the one in particular that caught my eye, was a very special train, *City of Truro* en route from York to Swindon.

I had never seen a 'City', although I had heard my father talk about them enough, as he had fired them for miles when he was a fireman. That was long before my time, and I was a little disappointed when *City of Truro* came rolling past the next morning in the half-light of a dirty March day. She looked dowdy with her side rods stacked in the tender, along with wooden packing cases, just another 'Bulldog' with big driving wheels, but I had not made allowance for the expertise of Swindon Works, where she was bound for, and they did a splendid job on her, as I realised. When I saw her next, a few months later, she was standing in the spur outside Didcot East Junction signal box. She was covering station pilot duties and I just had to wait for her to come into the station. When she arrived, I was soon up on the footplate, having a good look at her; she had been painted, her nameplate was restored and she was as new as the day she was born. I would have loved to have fired her, not just shunting up and down, but on a train running free as she was meant to, and from that casual remark, I began to wonder if plans could be laid. It had been a long time since I had used a shovel, and this little locomotive was no 'County'; her firebox was the same as a 'Bulldog', and her little tender was the same size as a Dean Goods, it should be easy, if only I could arrange it.

'In this world there is nothing for the dumb', that's what my old dad used to say, and I've found it to be true, but the way things fell into my lap was, on this occasion, a combination of circumstances. Firstly, with my being in Didcot instead of miles down the line, and secondly, walking into my old footplate mate Ted Hurle. From the conversation (after we had finished hugging each other) emerged the fact that during the next week, he was working the 12.42p.m. Didcot to Southampton, and the engine booked for the job was *City of Truro*. With that information, it was up to me to do something. I was booked in Sandford box that week, but I did have a day owing, and also an understanding wife, thank goodness. What I was attempting was sheer pleasure, if I could pull it off, but a lot of arranging had to be done, and the first thing was to apply for a day off. Bill Checkley liked to have a good reason on any application for a day, so I gave it to him, namely that I was going to fire *City of Truro* but he didn't believe me, nevertheless, he did grant me the day off. The next step was to go down to the shed and see the foreman and square him. He was most sympathetic, he would love to allow me to fire her, and if it was up to him I could, but (and there is always a 'but') I was no longer a member of the locomotive department, indeed, I hadn't been for years, and neither was I still a member of the Footplate Union, so there was a problem there. However, he could give me a pass to travel on the footplate as an observer, and once out of sight, if I did just happen to pick up the shovel, then he wouldn't know anything about it, so long as I didn't shout it about, and didn't turn up in overalls. So I arranged it for the Thursday, and brought my wife and children to my mother's house in Didcot, where we could all stop overnight and return home the next morning, which would give me plenty of time to pick up the late turn at Wolvercote sidings, and that was the way it worked out.

The next day I slid through the station entrance, turned right and ran up the steps onto number one platform, and there, standing in the Newbury bay, were four coaches with *City of Truro* at the head. I saw Bill Checkley walking towards me, and he told me that I must be mad to spend a day firing a steam engine, and I agreed with him, I *was* mad, but so must he be also, to go crawling into bushes to get briars for his roses! At all events he was satisfied, but knowing that I was one for a leg-pull he had thought that my reason for wanting a day off was one; now he knew that for once I was genuine.

There was a short toot on the whistle so I began to run, as Ted was obviously ready to leave. I sprang into the cab just as the engine began to move, Ted beaming with pleasure at the sight of his old fireman from years ago, back on the footplate with him once more, and I grinned back, delighted to be there, then I got up into the corner of the cab out of sight until we were past the pilot engine and the signal box.

Ted pointed to a carrier bag hanging on the cab hook and I opened it and took out an overall jacket and trousers, and by the time we were passing the milk depot and onto the branch, I was dressed ready to start work. I looked over the side expecting to see the side rods flashing round, as they would have been, by now, on a 'Bulldog', but they were going over in such a lazy manner it was hard to believe that we were keeping time. It was a situation which I found hard to accept, as I was on the familiar 'Bulldog' footplate but with the wheels of a 'Castle' going round outside, and there was none of the haste that I remembered so well. We seemed to be floating, and it was a surprise to see Ted shut off and wind down the screw reverser ready to run into Upton; a couple of brisk shots on the vacuum brakes saw her gliding into Upton station, and with one final burst she stopped.

Ted's fireman was known as Johnnie; I can't remember his surname now, but I can remember what a good lad he was, and he suggested that the guard might like his company, which would give me a bit of room on the footplate, so he jumped off onto the platform and left me to it. After a break of ten years, the old combination was together again, Ted and I looked at each other, the look of sheer pleasure of two old mates enjoying the situation, as we felt that we had put the clock back, and for those few hours we were going to savour every minute. There was a blast on the whistle back down on the platform and Ted hurriedly blew off the brakes, we had been so wrapped up in each other he had not noticed the time, but now we were off, hitting the bridge with our exhaust, then into the start of the chalk cutting, Ted winding her back slowly on the reverser so that she would not pick up her heels. My goodness, it was good to be alive on this beautiful summer day, to see the sun shining in a blue sky, and the lushness of the green fields, and to sense the warmth of comradeship which we had for each other flooding across the footplate. I dropped the flap and left it down as I fired her, just the same as a 'Bulldog', well up at the back end to slope down towards the front of the firebox, the tongues of flame rolling and curling up with each

110

shovelful over the top of the brick arch. She began to whisper at the safety valve, so I put on the right hand live steam injector (she was steaming so freely there was no need to use the exhaust one). I lifted the flap, pulled down the tip-up seat and sat down to watch those slender six foot eight and a half inch wheels go round. She was not climbing up this bank in the manner that I remembered, she was striding, with the slow easy gait of a 'twenty-nine'. I watched the water in the gauge glass climb up out of sight then I shut off the injector and fired her some more, the shovel matching my mood and that of this lovely old lady, slow easy movements, sliding the shovel in the coal, turning round to slide it over the firehole ring, twisting my wrist in the old well-remembered way, scattering the coal all round the firebox.

I sat down again and had a good look at the boiler front. Swindon had really made a good job of her, with the deep green paint on the cladding, all the copper and brass pipes burnished, the gauge frame and the sight feed lubricator, up in Ted's corner, shot-blasted clean, the brass plate engraved with the valve cut-off on the reverser shining like gold. Even the ejector had been cleaned off, and the wooden handles of the brake and injectors had been varnished, I had never been on a footplate like it before, it was a show place. We cleared the bank with the water in the glass dropping half way down as we came onto the level, and I put the injector on again, no more firing was needed for the moment. Ted tapped down the regulator until she was riding on the jockey valve and wound her back, nearly into mid gear, and then she began to fly, racing across the top of the Downs, leaning over slightly into the gentle curve through Churn Halt, flying gracefully with the wind, running with the smoothness of a race horse. There was no rattling or bucking, and every bolt in her frame and cab was tight, in other words, she was perfection.

With the bit between her teeth, *City of Truro* seemed to run for ever, and this occasion was certainly the nearest that I had ever been to feeling that a locomotive was really alive, but alas, she had to be held back as Compton station was growing larger with each turn of those slender tall wheels. Ted gave her a good long burst on the vacuum brake, and as his hand grasped the handle and pushed it over, the air roared harshly in and she reared back, almost as if he had reined in a galloping horse, then the vacuum pump took over and she rolled sedately into Compton.

City of Truro began to blow off gently as we stood in Compton station. Despite that leisurely gait up the bank from Upton, the run through Churn had made us two minutes early, so she had to stand there with the slight blow from the cylinder drain cocks giving the impression that she was straining forward, eager to get moving again. Then we were away once more, Ted opening and closing the cylinder cock lever and sealing the blow, while I dropped the flap again and fired her all round the box, packing the back corners and under the fire hole doors where it had burnt hollow, and as I slid the shovel back into the coal we were swooping down into Hampstead Norris, the blower on slightly to clear the smoke, and I realised that after the long lay-off I was beginning to forget the distances between the various stations.

As she pulled away she began to 'lose her feet', giving a quick 'cha cha' out of the chimney before Ted could shut her down, then she picked up and began to gallop up the bank towards Pinewood Halt, which was not an easy place to stop because it was on the curve and difficult for the driver, but I remembered the drill, and Ted let her drift in with the brakes just rubbing whilst he watched my hand as I waved him down. I leaned far out of the cab until the coaches were almost in the Halt, then when I gave my hand signal to stop there was a 'woosh' as the vacuum brake was applied and we had arrived.

No more firing was needed for a while, and after what seemed like a few turns of the wheels, we arrived at Hermitage for a one minute stop. Then we needed a little bit of steam, just enough to get her rolling, and it was just a matter of letting her free-wheel down the long drop into Newbury, running level with the roof-tops of the houses, drifting over the Bath road and under the bridge where we waved to the signalman at Newbury East Junction (he had come to the window to admire this resplendent lady). Then Ted brought her speed down sharply as we came off the branch and on to the main line, letting her run, just ticking over until we felt the kick of the facing points, then a little steam brought us into Newbury station.

We were booked to stop here for thirty-five minutes, so as soon as the station work was done, we pulled forward and filled the tank at the water column, then went up and over the points, to back into the Down bay, leaving the platform clear for the next train. As soon as we came to a stand, I dropped the flap and the back damper down one notch and began to pull forward some coal. She stood there in the sunlight, gleaming in her red and green paint, the sun sparkling from the safety valve bonnet, the copper band round her chimney taking on a blue tint from the heat, and the famous nameplate curving over on the frames proudly acclaiming her name to her admirers, who were a dozen small boys, all very excited by the sight of her.

At 2.00p.m. we were off again, and I lifted the damper and let the fire brighten up until the Lambourn branch began to drop away on our right, then I started to fire her again as she galloped towards Enbourne Junction. The vacuum siren gave a 'whoop' as we hit the A.T.C. ramp at Enbourne's Distant signal. Ted lifted the cancel trigger and eased her down a bit, then there was a lurch and we swung away from the main line and on to the Winchester branch, and then she was working hard up the bank towards Woodhay.

It all came flooding back to me now, the engines that I had worked on this line so many years ago, such as the big American 2-8-0s, where were they now, I wondered, and the L.M.S. 8Fs and the many 'Halls', 'Granges' and all the others. Now, by sheer luck, I was firing *City of Truro*, an engine that had been tucked away for years while all my footplate years slipped by, but I realised that my old dad had been right, these 'Cities' were good engines, and I asked myself why on earth were they ever done away with?

It was ironic in a way, time on the old Winchester branch seemed to have stood still while I had been away, and yet Woodhay, Highclere, Burghclere, Litchfield, Whitchurch, Sutton Scotney, Worthy Down and Kings Worthy all slipped past so quickly on this particular day, and we were gliding into the tunnel to pull up gently to a halt in Winchester Chesil station. We stopped only two minutes here, just enough time to uncouple the horse-box that had been coupled on at Newbury, leaving it in the station for the pilot to collect, then we commenced the fifteen-minute run down into Eastleigh. That big busy station was simply bustling with movement in sharp contrast to the sleepy country stations which we had just left. Big Southern locomotives burst through to flash by, their coaches roaring behind them, and the Up expresses fresh out of Southampton, hammered up through the station, they were almost enough to make our little lady shy-off.

We stood simmering in the station, posing for the numerous devotees with their cameras. Grown men, serious with intent, not for them the schoolboy chatter, but soon the guard's whistle sent us on our way. I could afford to sit down now, and bask in the tribute given by the Southern lads as they looked up and saw us marching by. Past the smoky engine shed, past the lines of dirty engines waiting to go through the Works and the half-dozen that had just come out, brilliant in their new colours, their wheels clean and sharp looking, side rods polished and buffers ebony black. They had been cleared of all the years of grime, and were now waiting to go back into service and unfortunately to renew that dirty mantle. The lads waved as they enjoyed the sight of this grand old lady striding south in the sunshine.

As we ran down the main line between Eastleigh and Southampton, I could see the changes that had been made since I was last this way. The rubble of bombed houses was gone, the bomb-sites had been cleared and new buildings had sprung up to replace the scars, and as we ran into the once dingy terminus at Southampton I found the station newly painted, and everything was bright and cheery in the sunshine. Johnnie emerged from the guard's van and uncoupled while I was placing a lamp on the tender, then the station pilot drew off our coaches and pulled up over the points. The points were then changed to allow us on to the turntable, whilst the coaches were shunted back into the platform which we had vacated.

Since we had arrived at 3.56 p.m. and were not due away again until 4.55 p.m. that gave us an hour to turn and top up with water and back on to our train, which allowed plenty of time for a cup of tea and a sandwich. By 4.25 p.m. we had finished, so while Ted and I went round with the oil-can, Johnnie shovelled some coal forward and I went round *City of Truro* with a handful of cotton waste, dry-wiping the dust of the journey from her boiler, keeping the sheen of her beauty from becoming soiled. I felt that I owed her this little bit of attention, for she had given me more pleasure in these last few hours than I would have thought possible.

At 4.55 p.m. we began the long trip home, and as we left, I looked back towards the terminus knowing that I would never again see Southampton from the footplate of a Great Western steam locomotive. We ambled back into Eastleigh for a two minute stop, then at 5.12 p.m. we left, swinging over the main line at Shawford and onto the branch up to Winchester and our home ground. I had stood behind Ted up from Southampton, just enjoying the sight of him handling this engine in the way that I well remembered. I didn't even watch Johnnie firing her, I was just content to soak in the enjoyment of being on the footplate again, but realising that each time those great big driving wheels went round it was drawing my illicit journey into the past, to a close.

Winchester was reached on time, and we stood in the station

watching the shop girls and workmen leave the train, weary from the day's work in Eastleigh and Southampton. The tunnel mouth showed as a black hole in front of us, and the tunnel itself curved away into the darkness as it burrowed under the big hill towering above us. Ted opened the ejector and blew off the brakes, then he told Johnnie to sit down and went over to the fireman's side to watch out for the guard. As the twin needles reached the 22lb mark on the vacuum and reservoir gauge I stepped forward and placed the handle in the upright position, and as I did so, Ted pulled the whistle chain, looked over at me with a smile on his face and said 'Right away, mate'.

Without even thinking, I opened the ejector again and lifted the regulator, the metal feeling smooth, warm and friendly in my hand, and *City of Truro* began to move, gently at first as I could feel the power going from that shining handle into the wheels. As her exhaust hit the tunnel mouth I gave her a little more steam and instantly the exhaust deepened and she began to stride deeper into the tunnel. I snapped down the clip on the reverser and held the fixed handle loosely in my hand, and very gently began to link her up, half a turn at a time, with the valves floating enough for me to feel them in my palm. We cleared the tunnel with her running strongly, one more turn and I clipped her down, the regulator stopping in the same position, then up went her nose and she began to bite into the bank, but just as she was beginning to run freely I had to close her down for Kings Worthy. I gave her a little shot on the vacuum brake just to get the feel of her braking, and as the blocks began to rub on the wheels I gave her a little more and she sauntered into the station and stopped. She stood there almost sniffing at the long climb ahead to Worthy Down, and just then Ted came over and told me not to treat her so gently, because she was built to take hills and dales in her stride. So when we set off once again, I gave her half regulator and wound her back as she began her march, matching the turns to her demands, then when she told me, in the way that all steam locomotives communicate to the driver (through the palm of the hand and the soles of the feet) that she was happy at this setting, I lifted the clip back in the ratchet and she was left alone to make her own way. I looked down at Ted doing the firing, feeding her with coal as he had taught me to do so long ago, little and often in the right place and at the right time, spraying and spreading, tucking it into the corner of the fire box, each shovelful darkening the plume of her exhaust. I felt a deep feeling of affection for this wonderful man who had enriched my life so much, and he must have read my thoughts, he looked up at me and smiled, we were so close again, we did not need to speak.

I shut off at the top of the bank and let her run, the gradient slowing her up for Worthy Down station, then a few turns of the wheels with steam on and she could free-wheel down in to Sutton Scotney, Ted leaning over the side of the cab to catch the cool air on his face, before the easy climb to Whitchurch, followed by the long drag up to Litchfield and beyond.

It was roller-coaster road now, swooping down from Burghclere running like the wind down the dip and through the bridge and up into Highclere where she stood waiting time almost panting with excitement until the time came to be off again.

At this point I handed back to Ted, satisfied beyond words that I had handled the regulator again, and happy to pick up the shovel and enjoy myself in feeding the fire. We ran into Newbury at 6.41 p.m., an hour and forty minutes out of Southampton and after the station work was over we pulled over the points and backed into the bay for a rest until 7.22 p.m. There was time to take water and have a last cup of tea. It was to be the last time for me when that tea can went into the firebox, the last one after thousands over the years, and the last one with Ted.

I rode on the fireman's seat when we left Newbury, watching the sun go down and our shadows flying over the fields beside us, past the old familiar stations, little homely country stations with a blanket of roses growing along the fences, the Great Western branch line in all its glory, basking in the warmth of a soft summer evening. As we ran down the bank from Upton I noticed that the fields of corn on the Didcot side were beginning to turn colour, a soft yellow haze, before the coming rich brown of harvest time reflecting back on the green of the polished boiler. As we swept under Hagbourne bridge the clock was put back nearly thirty years as my dear wife and children waved to me from the same spot as I used to wave to father on the old 'Skylark'. We then floated round the curve and over Fleet Meadow bridge, the flanges squealing on the tight curve, a little steam into her cylinders, enough to clear the points, and then she slid into the bay platform at Didcot and arrived at her journey's end.

I still see *City of Truro* now and again in the museum at Swindon, but she is now cold and silent, clinically clean, the tender vacuumed out, new fire irons in the tender rack, an unblemished shovel and coal pick clipped so neatly in the cab, no oil drips and no warm comforting smell of an engine in steam. She is dead, as dead as *Lode Star* and the little Dean Goods, but, perhaps one day, they might all come out again. Perhaps it is wishful thinking to see a Churchward 'forty' marching out of Swindon station, followed by *City of Truro* and the Dean Goods with the 94 tank barking her head off, but stranger things have happened and I can only wish that this may happen one day.

To have to go back to work in the signal box the next day was a bit of a comedown, and I was silent and withdrawn for a couple of days. Had it been a good idea to try to recapture the past or should I have left things alone? But then, the demands of my signalman's training came to the fore, but for how much longer it would assert its pull, I didn't know. Each week saw more resignations going in from the lads, and it seemed that our old railway was dropping apart, and I too was beginning to think that perhaps I owed my family a better life.

I finished up the week at Wolvercote sidings and took over the late turn at Didcot North Junction the following week, and that was when the die was cast. The only way to this big box from my home at Kennington was to go by road to Appleford, and then to walk up the line to Didcot, so on the Monday afternoon, I parked my old Norton behind Appleford box and prepared for the walk, when Bill Prior of the marrow incident stuck his head out of the window and asked me if I was aware of the opportunities only a few miles away at the Morris Motors car factory. It seemed from his information that his son-in-law had joined the security staff there working the same hours as we were doing but for five pounds a week more, plus a pension and pay, when off sick. I had not been aware of this, in fact, it seemed almost too good to be true, the sick pay certainly sounded interesting, because I knew that if I went off duty sick, my money would stop the minute that I walked out of the signal box, so this information seemed to be worth investigating.

I wrote to the factory for an interview and a couple of weeks later I was called to attend, and I found everything that I had been told was true. I left that interview to discuss things with my wife, and although she knew that the railway was my life, that extra money and the conditions that went with it, were an opportunity not to be missed. To cut a long story short, I accepted the job, and gave Bill Checkley a month's notice. Bill was most upset to hear that yet another man with the district 'under his hat' wanted to leave, but he had to face the fact that £9. 8s. 0d a week was not much for the responsibility of being able to work all those signal boxes.

It was pure coincidence that my last three weeks as a signalman took me back to Milton where my career had begun ten years before. With the introduction of colour light signals and power signal boxes, it would not be long before there would be no more Milton or any other manual signal boxes. Progress had caught up with me again, and I could see that given a few years, I would be either stuck in a power box where I would never actually see a train, or land up (as so many lads did) on the platform as an inspector, neither position really appealing to me. The third alternative was to be made redundant, so it was obviously time to get out while I was still young enough to learn another trade. My last turn of duty was on Saturday, July 26th 1958 and the last train that I dealt with was the 9.18p.m. stopping passenger train from Didcot to Swindon, a fitting end for a Didcot signalman to pass on a Didcot-crewed train!

I cycled up the path towards Foxhall for the last time with sadness in my heart, thinking about nearly twenty years of railway work behind me. On the following Monday I began work as a security officer at Morris Motors at Cowley and in the years that followed, I found that all the railwaymen who had gone to Morris's before me (and there were many) had not stood still, but like good railwaymen had found that there is always another step to climb. Ten years later I was the supervisor, and then the final avenue opened up and I became an engineering investigator, and for once, I reckon that I will stand still and settle for that.

Some time after I had left the footplate, the other lads who had left said that they had no regrets, and the same was repeated to me by the lads who had stayed in railway service. In reality, of course, there must be regrets, for the railway that I knew in my youth, although perhaps not for the railway of colour light signals and diesel locomotives.

It was a long time before I held a shovel in my hand again, on 26th May, 1975 on *King George V* at Hereford, and several years were to pass before I would have the chance for a footplate run. Then one Sunday in August 1980, I had a day out and visited the Bluebell Railway, and there I ran into a wonderful lot of understanding lads who quickly kitted me out with a cap and overall jacket, together with a footplate pass, then I was escorted onto the footplate of the beautifully restored Adams' radial tank No. 488 and invited to 'have a go'.

It gave the lads a good laugh to see an ex-Great Western man firing a London and South Western Railway locomotive, but I fired her from Sheffield Park to Horsted Keynes in just the same way as I had always fired a locomotive, and the injectors worked the same way so nothing was really any different. The surprise came when we got back to Sheffield Park and I started to make my farewells. Those lads would have none of it, as I had proved that I could fire this little engine, but they asked if I was still good enough to *drive* her? I could scarcely ignore this challenge, so I placed her in full fore gear, pushed over the regulator and marched her up the bank as if I had never been away.

I've joined the Bluebell now, and who knows, one day I might get the chance to fire the 'Schools'.

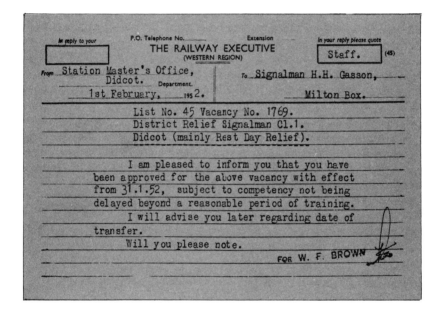

GREAT WESTERN RAILWAY.

(1406)

APPLICATION FOR SIGNALMAN'S BONUS.

No. _7811_

Signalman _James Jardine_ having performed six months' duty in the _____ Cabin at _Didcot_ Station, without having made any mistake in working Points, Signals, or Block Telegraph, or having committed any other act, or made any omission, which might have led to an accident, applies for his Bonus, and is entitled to it in accordance with the conditions shewn on the other side.

The authorized Bonus for this Cabin is at the rate of £ _5—0—0_ per annum.

Half-yearly Instalment of £ _2.10.0_ due on _Jany 3rd_ 18_92_

Previous Bonus was due on* _July 3rd 1891_

Jackson .... Sub-Inspector of Division.

_____ .... Chief Inspector of Division.

_____ .... Superintendent of Division.

* If the Bonus has been deferred from any cause, the particulars must be stated here, giving the date of the offence.

CONDITIONS.

1. If a Signalman is off duty for more than a month by illness, his bonus must be deferred for a period equal to the time of his illness.

2. The portion of bonus money earned shall be allowed in cases of Signalmen dying before the expiration of the bonus half year, as well as in the case of those promoted or transferred to other grades, or incapacitated and unfit for further duty, provided they have worked for three months without having any serious irregularity recorded against them in connection with the working of the Block Telegraph Points and Signals, and affecting the safety of the Line;

3. Signalmen, who are promoted during their bonus half-year from less important to more important Cabins, will receive a proportionate amount of the increased bonus paid at the more important Cabin, dating from the time of transfer, thus:—If a Signalman is one month at a £3 Cabin, and five months at a £5 Cabin, he will receive for the half-year £2 6s. 8d.

4. To be entitled to receive a bonus, a Signalman must have performed six months' duty, without having made any mistake in working Points, Signals, or Block Telegraph, and without having committed any other act or made any omission which has or might have led to an accident. Should he be guilty of any such act he will lose his bonus for the period between the date upon which his previous bonus became due and the date of the offence, from which latter date his next half-yearly bonus will commence to run.

Waterlow and Sons Limited, Printers, London Wall, London.